# A CLIP OF STEEL

TO JULIA

We are such stuff as dreams are made of . . .
(Shakespeare, *The Tempest*)

*In the sense of the quotation, all the characters in this book,*
*including myself, are entirely fictitious*

# Chapter One

This thing of darkness I acknowledge mine.

SHAKESPEARE, *The Tempest*

In 1810 when Mauritius was annexed from France by Britain its population comprised at least five races. But in addition to the dominant French, the Dutch, Chinese, Indians and Africans were those of mixed blood.

Because of the smallness of the island and its remoteness from Europe this dusky fringe tended to increase, and those of a comparatively white skin feared the encroachment. Consequently that tendency to paranoid obsession shared by most human beings found a convenient quarry in the Creole and Eurasian. Social status was determined not so much by wealth, wit or achievement as by a pigment of the skin; whether one was black, white, yellow or khaki.

My great-grandfather, Captain Blackburn, was an officer in the English force which invaded the island. He married Jeanette de l'Ecluse, the daughter of a French officer whose family had been on the island for many years. Of their four sons my grandfather, Charles, was the second. He experienced a religious vocation and after a period in London, where he qualified as an Anglican priest, returned to his native island. There he spent the greater part of his life, though his adventurous pastoral duties also entailed visits to the neighbouring lands of Seychelles and Réunion. A photograph of him as a young man is reminiscent of some character of Dostoevsky. Fanatical eyes smoulder under a high forehead, the nose is aquiline, the mouth petulant, sensitive and sensual.

Grandfather married on the island, but in the case of Grandmother Elise, a Scottish strain was added to the Mauritian blend. Perhaps it endowed her with that common sense which was her especial virtue. She must have needed every scrap of it to cope with the vagaries of her husband and the climate. The stories my father told me of his childhood in Ravineside were of hair-breadth escapes. Wild nature, black magic and disease could only be circumvented by prayer, watchfulness and chastity.

The latter was preserved by a large tin bath which was kept on the veranda outside Grandfather's bedroom and filled each evening with cold water by the servants. Into this he would leap when assailed at night by the shafts of Eros. The God's daytime assaults were circumvented by digging. The large hole which he made every week or so in the rear compound had a purely thera-peutic value, since it was filled in on each occasion. However the unpredictability of the Mauritian fauna and climate was less easy to cope with. Children died of malaria, poisonous snakes would unroll with the Venetian blinds and ('Quick, my boy, the large cleaver!') be held writhing on the kitchen table until dispatched with a neat downstroke. There were rabid dogs and Uncle Mark only escaped the consequence of a bite from an infected animal by cauterizing his wound with a red-hot poker. My father could still remember the reek of singeing flesh. On another occasion, clinging to a kitchen door, Grandfather was borne aloft by a hurri-cane.

As Protestant pastor he was the especial target of 'Petit Albert', a virulent cult of black magic. Sorcerers with oiled bodies and sharp knives attempted his life, and insinuated powdered glass into the family soup tureen. Not only were their attempts unsuc-cessful but while escaping from Ravineside in the form of a pig, one unfortunate magician was shot by Grandfather in his front left trotter. On the next day this unenlightened native carried his arm in a sling. My father was convinced that sexual congress took place between the disciples of Petit Albert and the domestic sow. While visiting some remote settlement, Charles heard a strange noise coming from a shed separated from the other buildings by a fence of unusual height and stoutness. Although a grunt, it had human undertones, and on entering the building his suspicions were justi-fied. The creature which crawled naked among offal, straw and excrement, though for the most part human, was snouted like a pig.

I am grateful to my father for these stories he told to me when I was a child. He believed them and so do I – with a grain of salt and allowing for the jaundiced eye with which he and Grandfather Charles regarded an 'unchristian' and fallen world. His tales confirmed my belief in the unfathomable strangeness of the human being and his environment. They also convinced me of the illogic of human convictions. For it is remarkable that my father who believed, at least until later life, in the absolute validity of the Thirty-Nine Articles, who was depressed if he saw a single magpie, or broke a mirror, and who rebuked his children if, having spilt salt, they failed to throw a pinch over their left shoulder, would nevertheless indulge in derisive laughter at the mention of psychic research, telepathy, or ghosts whose haunt was in Europe.

This was characteristic of the man; he had a singular unwillingness to become conscious of his fears and fantasies, to yield them the lucidity of understanding. He was also anxious to believe that the powers of darkness were not related to himself, his thoroughly 'English' wife, or a Northumbrian vicarage, but confined to a few small islands of the Indian Ocean. However it is not possible to localize our ghosts.

Grandfather Charles was also an adept at wishing away the darker side of himself, his ghost, on to other people. His particular scapegoats were Roman Catholics and Eurasians. I am uncertain what caused his hatred of Rome, but the hatred was of extreme virulence. Indeed, when a grand-daughter who had come under his care after the death of her parents became engaged to a French lawyer of impeccable colour but the wrong faith, he subjected her to such a barrage of prayer and imprecation that she lost two stone and her fiancé. It was a dubious victory. Two months later, immunized against her Grandfather's denunciations, she married an Indian parson. Grandfather died before this union achieved its mixed blessings. However, my father carried on the tradition and steadily refused to meet his second cousin when she settled in England, or her seven admirable children. It is true that after the death of her Indian husband and of my mother he suggested that cousin Louise might become his housekeeper. But by then he was crippled with arthritis, and, as he remarked, when I suggested the rapprochement was a trifle belated, 'My boy, necessity knows no law!'

Two of my great-uncles refused to worship that racialism which was a religion of Mauritius. By marrying women whose skin was of a slightly darker shade than their own, these men were cut off from the European community as by an insuperable and contagious disease. The planter's widow married by Uncle Junius was both handsome, educated and wealthy, indeed she had loaned money to Charles, and on easy terms, for the purchase of Ravine-side. However, good looks, intelligence and generosity did not mitigate the evil of her mixed blood. Junius had married a Creole. Consequently his relationship with grandfather's family and the bulk of the European community suffered a change which though caused by psychic obsession and not the microbe of leprosy was no less drastic. On that island intimacy with one's own race was destroyed by miscegenation; what remained was, at best, a formal politeness chilling and sterile.

In his later years my father told me with deep feeling of his shock and disgust when grandfather Charles announced to the assembled family that another uncle, my namesake, Thomas, had married a coloured woman, and henceforth must be dead to his relations. This beloved and respected man – he was I believe an Inspector of Schools – was neither to be asked to the house, saluted in the streets nor mentioned in conversation. His name was solemnly expunged from the family Bible, a form of exorcism not uncommon on the island. However, Thomas was restored to his family after some eighteen months. The malaria parasite which permanently removed his wife from Mauritius was considered a blessing in disguise by all but the unfortunate bridegroom.

If marriage with an Indian, Eurasian, Chinese, or Creole could isolate one from friends and family as effectively as a pestilence, it was a catastrophe to be dreaded. In the case of my father the shared obsession of the white community was made particularly painful by a chance of heredity. Of all his family he alone had been touched by the Evil One; I mean possessed certain physical characteristics that could be associated in those witch-hunting islands with the Eurasians. If I feel sympathy for myself as a small boy under his curious ministration, then I must also pity my father's childhood. Grandfather, though of a romantic, somewhat Russian appearance, had that hallmark of Mauritian respectability, a pair of blue eyes. Grandmother was a very decent shade – so were the girls. As for the younger son, Edward, nature had blessed him with such Teutonic blondness and squareness of jaw that he was employed as a secret agent during the 1914-18 War and received a Military Cross for bravery. Only my father suggested the possibility of some Indian or Creole ancestor by a somewhat dusky skin and a certain indefinable quality of mouth and nostril.

Perhaps the climax of his childhood suffering was reached when he overheard a conversation between his twin sisters.

'Let's have a tea-party on Thursday,' one of them remarked, 'then Eliel will be at his Latin class and won't be able to come. He's so dark!'

No doubt that was but one detail from a whole climate of overheard conversations and quizzical expressions which gave to my father a sense of being haunted and isolated from his fellows. Twist and turn as he would the shadow followed. The evil could not be exorcized, only forestalled by masks of rectitude, innumerable gestures of reassurance, and ceremonies resembling those magic techniques which ward off the evil eye.

If the relationship between father and son had been less intimate then Eliel might have defied that racial Moloch of whom Grandfather Charles was, in some sense, the High Priest. Edward, who regarded his father with cool distaste, seems to have done so, though he was packed off to England before his marriage to an Indian student could take place. For Eliel no such revolt was possible since the 'love' between him and his father was both obsessive and tenacious. As a boy he would rise repeatedly from his bed and crouch on the mat outside Charles's bedroom door to catch the sound of breath and be reassured that his beloved was still living. Doubtless such a preoccupation with the man's death suggests a wish for it to happen. But 'love' can be strengthened, or rather changed into servitude, if no admission is made of the hatred with which it is so often allied. Because he would not admit its strand of fury, the rope which bound Eliel to Charles was unbreakable. Consequently my father could not deny the racial obsessions of Charles. I do not think my grandfather ever overtly criticized the appearance of his son. On the other hand, quite apart from the hints of his sisters and school acquaintances, any pocket mirror could confirm Eliel's worst suspicions. He himself might be contaminated by the very evil condemned with bell, book and candle by his beloved father.

I believe he escaped from this dilemma by an operation upon his personality considerably more drastic than the amputation of a limb. Since he loved Charles, he could not deny the man's obsessions, sound currency anyway in the island. So he denied both his rejection of Charles and the conviction – no less real for being irrational – of his own evil. Doing this, and with a surgical thoroughness, he cut himself off from the source of his inward life, from the possibility of self knowledge and the exorcism of his ghosts. Those ghosts still existed, but outside him now, in the external world. The operation brought about a partial blindness or rather a fault of vision. Now he could see plainly outside in others, above all in myself, his first son, just those emanations of darkness which as a quality of himself he could not bear.

It was necessary for him to be the white child whom Charles loved, so I must be the black one and carry his somewhat tarstained cross. I was his son though and he would do what he could to redeem me. The start of his process of redemption is one of my first memories.

There is a silver tray. Some slices of lemon are on it, a bottle of hydrogen peroxide and a few tufts of cotton wool. It is about seven o'clock in the bedroom of a north country vicarage, and I am six years old. Tray in hand and with an air of uneasy devotion, my father is seated beside me on the bed. What he wants, with only six years to my credit, is quite beyond me. I can sense his unease though and that when he says, 'Well, my boy, and what have you been doing today?' he is quite uninterested in the fact that I climbed a small elm and made a lavatory with a piece of old drain pipe and a flower pot. But he's looking at me now and with a very strange expression.

'Tommy, you've been out in the sun and it's been a hot day, so

I'm going to put some of this on your face. It will make it better.'
Although I could feel the sting of the lemon and peroxide with
which he smeared my face, as to what 'It' was, in those early years
I had no clue. I do know that when Mother came in during one of
our rituals I resented both her protests and intrusion. She didn't
realize that Father and I were working on something together,
working to get me right. It was only years later that I realized he
had been working to create that deep self-mistrust which is still my
companion. However there is a positive side to traumatic experience: the mistrust I gained from my father made for turbulence
but also fostered a need for self-exploration. I had to unravel his
bad dream if I was to get clear of it.

Even in those early days from time to time I did see through
those evening rituals of Father and realize that they were very
nasty indeed. But a child has no one to back his judgment and
confirm that a parental obsession is not the natural climate of an
adult world. Nor can he write to some understanding official, 'Sir,
I find the parent supplied thoroughly unsatisfactory, please supply
a more reasonable alternative, and at your earliest possible conve-
nience.' He must adjust to the only reality he has got at whatever
price, or reject what is, and roll away into the no-man's-land of
madness.

One can blame the past. But where does the blame start? It was
my father's own childhood experience that made it inevitable he
should wish on to myself the guilty shadow he associated with
the Eurasian. The very thoroughness, the evangelical fervour with
which he conducted a mission against that shadow, is reminiscent
of Grandfather Charles. The bleaching ritual was only part of the
process by which I was to be brought to a whiter than whiteness
and, weaned of my cockerel bones, snakeskin and bladder-stick,
enter the mission hut in calico trousers and sweat shirt to the tune
of 'Onward Christian Soldiers'.

However, the projection of my father's condemned areas on to
other people was by no means perfect. In later years, though insu-
lated from Mauritius by a canonry in a northern cathedral, three
framed testimonials from the grateful parishioners of his previous
living and the signed photograph of a British general, he suffered

agonies of shame when entering a hospital to be operated on for gall-stones. He was not worried about the result of the operation. His penis and scrotum were of a darker shade than the rest of his body. This would be observed by the nurses.

The extent to which his obsession had remained unchanged by the reality of a long life was shown to me by a visit that two of the children of his cousin Louise paid to him when in retirement at Bournemouth. These Eurasians would not have been asked to the house by invitation, but since they arrived at the door without warning, they were entertained with tea and embarrassed silence.

The eldest, Jeanette, was teaching chemistry in a London grammar school while her younger sister, after completing a degree at some university, was a research chemist. Both in their appearance, intelligence and sensitivity it is difficult to believe they did not combine the more pleasing aspects of their European and Asiatic descent. Father's myopic eye gained a different impression.

'They were all wrong,' he declared, 'all wrong. The seed hadn't mixed properly.'

'What about Barbara?' I asked.

'Barbara was all right, poor child, quite all right.'

Barbara, my first cousin, was the daughter of my mother's sister, June, and her husband Edward. She was of a cheerful disposition. I remember here whoops and yells of delight during the final 'Gallops' of those Hunt Balls which my Aunt insisted Barbara should attend – to the vast embarrassment of her sisters and cousins. I remember her feeding alternate chocolate drops and pebbles to a docile retriever. As a little boy I remember her standing up naked in the bath covered with soap suds, crowing like a cock, and I remember the statement of Wordsworth that the lives of idiots are 'hidden with God'; for Barbara was a Mongoloid idiot and though she lived to the age of twenty-six never grew up. Perhaps she was neither 'Right' nor 'Wrong' but to my aged father she corresponded, because of her unblemished European descent, to some indefinable standard of rectitude which his Eurasian nieces, despite their beauty and academic achievements, were powerless to attain.

# Chapter Two

Orestes: You don't see them – but I see them.
They are hunting me down. I must move on.

Aeschylus, *Choephoroi*

My father left Mauritius when he was eighteen. He was to qualify as a priest, then come back to help Charles on the island. No doubt his failure to return, despite many hints and entreaties, was over-determined and had little connection with his overt explanations in terms of health and money.

As they said goodbye on board ship at Port Louis, Charles presented my father with a small red notebook which he kept by him to the end of his life. This closely written and rather moving document expresses a concern with Eliel's welfare that is hag-ridden with anxiety. It catches the sense my father had to the end of his days of being thrust, powerless and vulnerable, into a universe with which he was linked by no shared energy or substance; a natural world bent on his destruction. The supernatural realm was no less hostile. There is scant suggestion in Grandfather's notebook of that Other who desires we have more abundant life, who cares for the sparrow and will companion us in the valley of death. The life of all living creatures may be a partial manifestation of God, but both Charles and Eliel attributed to the Deity their own mistrust of vitality and passion. In consequence, their affirmation of God was a denial of his manifestation in the created world. A cross between a hanging judge and the chairman of a Cornish watch-committee, their God, like Caliban's Setebos, regarded his creation with profound disapproval. He only tolerated those actions and sentiments of his children which denied the spontaneous life within them and were directed towards a vacant heaven, neatly capsuled off from the zest of living.

'My boy, watch and pray! Remember you were born with an

extremely delicate constitution and must take the greatest care of your health. The body is the temple of the Holy Ghost; do not defile it. Every night I will say, "Sleep well my boy, God bless you", and every night you must say after your prayers, "Good night, Papa, God bless you". Avoid fried food and uncooked vegetables. God is not mocked; the Devil goeth about like a roaring lion to devour us. The price of uncleanness is death. See that your lamp is kept burning.'

Such exhortations are followed by practical medical advice. The suggested remedies are drastic. Indeed, my father must have been blessed with an iron constitution to have weathered for over eighty years the incessant drenchings of castor-oil, cascara and bromide by which he warded off the evil eye and abused his stomach.

Despite the hazards that beset him Eliel was ordained priest in Durham Cathedral, but instead of returning to Mauritius took up a curacy in the parish of Wolsingham. It is difficult to imagine a greater contrast to his volcanic and tropical birthplace than this village of the Wear Valley of Durham with its moorland farms, pinewoods and peaty streams. It is even harder to think of a stock more different to the Blackburns in heredity, temperament and appearance than the principal family of this dale.

The Fenwicks take their name from the Anglo-Saxon 'fen wicker', dweller in a fen. I very much doubt whether the Weardale Fenwicks would ever have left the first fens they lived in if it had been a question of choice. However, once driven reluctantly over the North Sea they took root as farmers in a few valleys of Northumberland and Durham. The Weardale branch of the family were not anxious to climb over the rim of their valleys into foreign parts. They were also unwilling to marry outside the family circle. Fenwicks, Muschamps, Kirsops and Bainbridges rang each other's changes from generation to generation. The result was a network of first, second and third cousins and a stock which preserved the reddish hair, jutting eyebrows and drooping bloodhound eyes of their ancestors. There was also an incidence of dullness slightly above the national average and a music as worthy and monotonous as the tune of Three Blind Mice.

Perhaps the height of the fortunes of the Weardale Fenwicks

was reached in the eighteenth century when they were Masters of the Hunt to the Bishops of Durham. The rock-bottom touched by a great-uncle of my mother, who kept a small but very successful store in the village of Stanhope. Their conviction that while farming was a worthwhile occupation trade most certainly was not may be a link with their Saxon forebears. Law one might also pursue, mining or the stock market. But there is scant record of a member of the family who followed letters, medicine or education – with the possible exception of the Reverend Charles Fenwick who fled the country in 1803 to avoid a charge of sodomy.

If one thinks of the Blackburns' god as a blue-eyed paranoiac in a clerical collar waging ceaseless war against sex, Roman Catholicism and the Eurasian then the Fenwicks might have worshipped a boulder. One of those gritty glacial lumps which are strewn over the moors where they shot grouse, and defy not Rome or the Half-Caste but Time itself. Of course if one takes the long view neither deity is likely to be successful. Still, one against Time, the other against the Powers of Darkness, like King Canute both of them were 'having a go'.

I think the Fenwicks' obsession with money and property came from their determination to control time and the process of change. If you didn't have lots of the stuff around you then Time – and long before Einstein they realized its spatial significance – would roll you out of your homestead, off and away in most unsuitable directions.

Many enemies beset this accumulation of money and farmland. Debauchery was one of them; so was art. At least the former did confirm their belief that the proper goals of life were tangible. But it was quite unsound as to what should be grasped. It was not a question of breasts and buttocks but of those deeds of ownership which cushioned the ribs with 'real' property. Art too often was an unlucrative obsession concerned not with current market values but some unsaleable dream. Its practitioners pushed an unreliable commodity and must be regarded with suspicion. At the age of seventeen my mother burnt the complete works of Lord Byron, the Christmas gift of a renegade uncle.

Since property furthered permanence it must be kept in the family. I suspect it was this desire for 'security' rather than any

Nordic mystique which prompted their inbreeding. My mother's sister Harriet was intended by the family to marry a kinsman of great wealth and so both augment her own considerable fortune and 'keep it within the family'. She had no liking for this dour mine-owner whose breath, a coachman remarked, 'could fell a man', and the process by which she was prised away from the engineer she loved and forced into an abhorrent marriage was of extreme cruelty. Two years after her marriage, and having given birth to one child, she deserted a world in which she could take no further interest.

At the time when my father took up his curacy in Wolsingham and intrigued the stolid dalesmen by his French accent and mannerisms, my mother's father, Thomas Fenwick, was exceedingly prosperous. This had not always been the case. The resources of the three or four moorland farms which supported my great-grandfather Heatherly and his family were severely strained by his addiction to children – there were twelve of them – and drink. Not that he was an alcoholic, but to the puritanical Wesleyan creed embraced by some of his relations any consumption of alcohol was excessive. There are stories of a shrewd white horse who would sustain her master by a nudge to port or starboard as he rode home from the public house. At other times on my grandmother fell the duty of retrieving him from the remote Phoenix Arms where he tended to stand large rounds of drink and, as a labour saving device, present the local butcher with a valuable bullock in exchange for a weekly meat ration.

At the age of twenty my grandfather became mining engineer in a Derbyshire colliery which belonged to one of his uncles. By industry and business acumen he eventually became a director and was able to buy a large house in his native village. However it was not until a maiden aunt left her fortune to Thomas and his children that the Fenwicks achieved that comfortable if not bloated affluence for which I have often been grateful.

The crucial event in the history of the family was the death of my grandmother, Anne, in her early forties. At the time the eldest daughter, Marion, was seventeen, while the youngest, my mother Adelaide, had reached the age of seven.

In early July a garden fête was to be held in a nearby village. Grandmother was to open it and decided she would be driven over in an uncovered dogcart. Just before driving away she asked Marion whether she should take a coat and, since the day was warm and cloudless, was told it would not be needed. Events proved my aunt wrong. On the return journey over a moorland road Grandmother was caught in a prolonged thunderstorm. She arrived home soaked to the skin and, complaining of pains in her back, went to bed. Pneumonia set in and after some ten days of ineffectual remedies her body was carried to its grave in Stanhope Churchyard. It is easy to forget that our personal fate and the fate of those around us depend on such minutiae: the failure to take a coat, an unusual accumulation of water vapour.

Partly because of the advice she gave, Marion developed an obsessive conviction that she was responsible for the death of her mother. To the dark colours of mourning she put on for the funeral she remained faithful until her own death. There was no question of marriage since on her lay the duty of supporting a bereaved father and his children. That she performed this duty with courage and devotion I know from my own experience of this remarkable woman, who offered to those related to her by blood and marriage a loyalty that was indifferent to ingratitude or irrational behaviour.

Not that Marion came unscathed from her bereavement. It confirmed her conviction that there was a quality within man himself, indeed in the very day-spring of existence which was irredeemably evil. This conviction she strengthened by readings of Schopenhauer and a collection of newspaper-cuttings concerned with every variety of disaster from earthquakes to child-murder and rape.

Because of her devotion to Grandfather and guilt at her mother's death, but also because it perpetuated the vicious cycle of existence, Marion entertained a hatred for the process of reproduction comparable to that of certain Eastern sects and early Christian Fathers.

'Nothing,' she once told me of marriage, 'nothing, Tommy, can make it right that a child should leave its own parents and go off with some complete stranger.' I recall the pinched venom of her mouth, her furious eyes as some girls in shorts and sleeveless blouses sauntered past us at the local agricultural show.

'They should all be strung up and flogged,' she muttered to herself and a puzzled nephew.

It was hard to reconcile the loving aunt I knew with the savage and sadistic puritan that possessed her and would denounce the maids, the gardener, any good-looking girl or woman who was not a relation. I see her standing in the porch of the house she built on a high shoulder of moorland. Her gardener is on his hands and knees. As he weeds between the cobbles of her large court-yard with a small pen-knife, she watches him with pleasure and malice. But this woman sustained my childhood and youth by her affection and understanding. No doubt her occasional outbursts of sadism were determined by the death of her mother. At times she would rage blindly at a catastrophe which had frozen – in part – 'the genial current of the soul'.

As if it had been cast into the life-stream of her family, Anne's gravestone conditioned the behaviour of her children and grand-children. For my mother this loss was particularly hard to bear because she was unable to share her grief with her elder sisters or father. For almost twenty years neither her mother's death nor life was ever mentioned, though photographs and a painting adorned the walls of the house and in a large wardrobe the coats and dresses of the dead woman were preserved from moths and corruption. What in old age recalled her bereavement was not a memory of the first nights of desolate crying but an incident which occurred some weeks after the funeral. She climbed on to her father's knee and nestled towards him. For a short time he tried to tell the small girl a story but unable to continue because of the sobs that muffled his voice, deposited Adelaide in a chair and left the room without explanation. Some moments later the governess informed her bereaved charge that she must never again sit on Mr. Fenwick's knee: 'It disturbs him!'

Grandfather believed he was protecting his children from the burden of his grief by never speaking of their dead mother. He was under a misapprehension. If suffering can be understood as the inevitable growing pains of our finite humanity then it has meaning and can be borne. By denying Adelaide the freedom of his grief he imprisoned her within her own sorrow. What could have been a road they travelled together, in pain, but towards a wider landscape, was associated with a prison cell. In such bondage she sweated out a grief that being solitary was guilt-ridden and hard to endure. From this searing and self-enclosed experience came her suspicion of passionate feeling, of any view of life mature enough to affirm life's tragic significance. As a child, she was not strong enough to endure her grief – alone. For much of her later life she tried to avoid emotion since for her pain and deep feeling were linked inseparably.

When she was a young woman, Adelaide had dark red hair, clear-cut features and blue eyes which gave the world an unusually direct and intimate appraisal. She was passionate although she feared passion. She shared the innate stoicism of her clan but lacked the emotional stolidity of those Fenwicks who regarded the Dionysian energies of life with grave suspicion. Dionysius could revel away in one night a whole month's earnings, had no roots and cared nothing for such worthy saws as 'Don't marry money but marry where money is' or 'Clogs to clogs in three generations'. Her concern with passion is suggested by her determination to marry a penniless curate of dubious family, whose accent, colouring and manner caused her relatives profound unease. However, she 'followed her heart'. It must have required considerable courage. Her second sister, my Aunt June, was the leader of the witch hunt against my unfortunate father. Watering her aggression with tears she announced that Adelaide was about to marry a coloured man and would give birth to black children. At this point my father made a neat move. He whisked up to Wolsingham two maternal uncles, the one a Wesleyan minister, the other a Harley Street specialist, but both rejoicing in the name of Anderson and a Scottish accent. The Fenwicks were duly impressed and the wedding went through without further opposition.

Children are like climbing plants. Not that they need a pole to grow round but they usually do need reasonably strong and affectionate parents if they are to become adult and not sprawl. If Eliel had been a more stable personality then Adelaide might have regained through marriage a greater measure of security and been able to bear her own strong feelings. However, although she would not admit this for many years, she must have realized after only a few weeks of marriage that in his personal life Eliel was unusually ambivalent and unpredictable. The instability of her husband, his strong but guilt-ridden sexuality, confirmed her suspicion of every variety of emotion whether its expression was sensual or poetic, and confined her even more rigorously to the surface of her personality. This separation of my mother from the deeper reaches of herself lasted until the final decade of her life. In those years, her persona started to melt as she drew nearer to death and she could express that imaginative passion which before I had only surmised under the hard crust of restraint. For the greater part of life she feared to feel deeply and see clearly. Her rigid limitation of emotion and vision may have determined in part my own anxiety which persists despite the passing of time and the increase of material security.

Whenever the conversation began to crackle with feeling and thought she would brush it aside with a remark about such safety devices as dogs, the weather, bluebells – or just a deep sigh.

'Tommy, dear, why must we talk about such depressing things when the world is full of so much beauty?'

God, death, sex, madness, cruelty, philosophy, any topic which savoured of strenuous thought and feeling and she would absent herself behind a curtain of platitude and disapproval. In the same way no doubt as Grandfather once absented himself from a small girl in her anguish.

These withdrawals of Mother made me believe (correctly, I suspect) that behind the minutiae of everyday existence was a mystery, dangerous, unfathomable, but infinitely exciting. It seemed that while drinking tea in the vicarage drawing-room, some neat curate or caryatid of the Mother's Union our guest, suddenly, acknowledged only by myself, the geiger counter would start to tick announcing the approach of the radio-active monster. The cups on the table seemed to shake. It was unmistakable. But no one dared to remark their shaking, listen to the noise under the floorboards, or turn his head to the French window and look

across the lawn where in the gathering dust an enormous troll
leaned between the yew trees.

It is not so much the difficulties of a childhood that are significant as the use we are able to make of them. From my dread – it
came in part from Mother's repression of thought and feeling –
I determined to penetrate beneath the floorboards and find out
what moved in that darkness. I must confront the shape on the
lawn and learn to name it. It is the repressions of our parents that
turn us towards self-exploration.

# Chapter Three

Let them not make me a stone and let them not spill me,
Otherwise kill me.                    Louis MacNeice

In 1912 my father was appointed to a living near the small mining
port of Whitehaven in Cumberland. Despite some domestic imper-
fections, he was a devoted priest and well-liked both by the miners
of his parish and the wealthier classes. He worked extremely hard
and raised enough money to build a new church of red sandstone
where his portrait may possibly still be seen in the vestry. The first
two years in Hensingham, before children arrived, were probably
the happiest in his life. At the home base Adelaide waited – and
there were no rivals. It was possible to brisk round so quickly from
miner's cottage to bazaar, country house, church service, parish
council that he kept a good length or so in front of his 'furies'.

The exceptional worldly innocence of this 'curer of souls' and
his wife is suggested by the name they gave their terrier pup. 'Pox'
had a nice sharp ring to it and resounded through the village till an
embarrassed verger suggested it was not entirely suitable. Mother
shared his ignorance of the facts of life. But I am still unsure of the
significance of a remark she made many years later when I was
pursuing with ardour and the worst intentions, a lapsed member
of her Girls' Friendly Society.

'I had him circumcised,' she informed an astonished friend, 'and
thought after that there'd be no trouble!'

Generalizations wilt before the complexity of people. How can
I reconcile my father's worldly ignorance and sexual guilt with the
advice he gave to a parishioner. An extremely fertile veterinary
surgeon, devoted to his wife, whisky and Evangelical Christianity,
inquired whether intercourse *per anum* during the 'unsafe period'
agreed with the Christian ethic.

'That,' said Eliel, 'is a matter between you and your Maker.'

When my father and his family left Hensingham for the living of Corbridge in Northumberland he took with him a silver salver engraved with the names of six churchwardens, an illuminated testimonial, and a beautifully bound book on whose vellum pages the signatures of more than two hundred parishioners bore witness to his virtues. Father had worked for this; but no external reassurance can lay our ghosts unless we ourselves in solitude conduct the hard ceremony of exorcism. In Mauritius, Eliel had undergone in an obverse way the mystic's union with God and felt himself made one with an evil that was inexplicable and all-embracing. Twist and turn as he might, still it remained, that contaminating experience. It determined much of his behaviour. It did not make it easy for his wife on whom lay the duty (and Adelaide was a stickler for duty) of protecting her husband from irrational terror and anxiety. Divorced by guilt from the reality of 'himself' from his vitality, his manhood, Eliel sought to avoid his misery by a complete at-oneness with his wife. He asked too much. Any other relationship of Adelaide, with her father, her sister, her children, even her dogs, was an attack and provoked extreme uneasiness.

Mother was very fond of dogs, particularly fox-terriers, a truculent and devoted breed who have still resisted the efforts of fanciers to change them into a hysterical canine oddity for 'points up' at Crufts. There was Mick, a sturdy rough-coated veteran who but for his long legs would have worked as assistant to a pack of foxhounds. I delighted in taking the creature for walks but he was never too tired to greet Eliel, as he returned from a round of visiting or the Parish Council, with a really nasty growl. As father came into the sitting-room, Mick would get up very slowly from the hearthrug, and hackles erect, walk stiffly to Mother's chair, growling his war-song. He would lay his nose between Adelaide's knees, and the doubleness of his expression, one eye motherward in dewy adoration, the other back at Eliel, bloodshot and venomous, was a feat of real ingenuity. Moreover, he managed, and at the same moment, both to smile and snarl. His motherward lip would droop ingratiatingly, but fatherward it rolled back at Eliel to expose a most effective set of canines. When the tension came to a head and to Mother's chant, 'Mick, Mick, come here! Eliel, can't you see he's frightened of you', they circled each other, one armed with a stick, the other a set of grip-teeth, I understood the affinity between a man and his dog.

Though devoted to her father, Mother could never visit him during his long and final illness without accusations more appropriate to adultery than the consolation of an aged parent. As my father's son I am a connoisseur of jealousy and can understand why she was unable to give expensive presents to her children without similar accusations.

Acting out in so many ways the role of a son, small and petulant, it was inevitable that Eliel should feel inferior to his wife and jealous of his children. He tried to dodge this inferiority by a recital of his successes in the parish which although to some extent true did not give him any real confidence. Mother's sycophantic chorus of 'What a headpiece! But don't be too masterful,' as he recounted how he got the better of some retired general or uppish grocer on the council, was distinctly irritating.

Defeated in an earlier game in which she was not the contestant, defeated in the double bed, if I may generalize from his remark, 'Poor girl, she never liked it', or from Mother's, 'No, Tommy, no decent woman gets any pleasure from it, it is a duty' (mind you, she must have done her duty with exceptional thoroughness since her last child was born when she was approaching fifty), in the other games she played with Eliel he must win. From long practice with her father she was an excellent chess-player and routed her husband in a few swift games. He would never again join her at the chess-board. Realizing his hatred of defeat, but convinced he was in need of healthy exercise, Mother would deliberately lob tennis-balls into the net to maintain his uneasy self-esteem. I was often puzzled by the power and accuracy of her back-hand drive against myself and its limp inefficiency against Father.

One cannot drop people back into the stream of life and see how they would react to other conditions of living. Whether or not in the karmic sense, we get the situation that is appropriate to us, we cannot be separated from those situations which make or – this latter may be more apparent than real – break us. No doubt if Adelaide had been in those earlier years a woman of greater self confidence and faced up to her husband's dominating insecurity then, after some uproarious temper tantrums, he might have withered into greater maturity. Or, who knows, lost his faith, his wife, his unreasonable reason!

Eliel was convinced his health was of extreme delicacy and this also was an effective weapon against his mother-wife. If she crossed him he would sink into an armchair with a groan, muttering 'my blood-pressure', 'my head' and produce an admirable series of palpitation. She seldom crossed him and was astounded when Uncle Daniel, a doctor, came to stay and after her inquiry, 'Do you think he will last another five years,' was informed:

'If you are referring to my nephew, he may live for ever; he's as strong as a horse!' After this she did grow sceptical and would at times do a 'clear-out' of the enormous medicine chest which made his room smell like a chemist's shop.

To the end of their lives my parents retained for each other a concern which if ambivalent was real. They were partners, united to outwit a world of whose bad intentions they were both convinced. But with great skill Eliel did extinguish, if not his wife's maternal tenderness, her romantic passion. The dead end of romance was reached when I suggested that a photograph of the young Eliel (he was in hospital at the time suffering from an overdose of the bromide he used as a tranquillizer) should be hung in her bedroom. 'No,' she said bitterly, 'I don't want to look at that now.'

When I was born, on the 10th February, 1916, she was aware of no flaw in his integrity. Little things have an incalculable effect on our destiny. Perhaps the word 'accident' is a synonym for 'inexplicable' and some providence manipulates for its purpose those details which often determine more rigorously the quality and direction of our lives than earthquake or the hardships of war. The detail which affected me was an abscess which developed on Mother's left breast after she had suckled me for some ten days. The right breast alone could not supply enough milk for a large and healthy baby and the proper course would have been to supplement my food with Glaxo or a similar preparation. I suspect it was her own childhood bereavement which determined my mother's devoted unwisdom in refusing to take this step. 'Hell,' says that admirable proverb, 'is paved with good intentions.' By insisting on breast-feeding her child against the wisdom of her own body, Mother associated my first nurture with pain, the infliction of pain, and deprivation. The source of life was tainted and inadequate. In the first few days a baby makes no distinction between its vitality and what sustains it, the mouth which sucks and the breast by which it is suckled. This first experience stained my feelings with a sense of corruption which seems indelible. However, if one's journey is necessary so no doubt are the particular events and fauna it offers. Much of my life has entailed an intricate threading of the recesses of the self in order to maintain some equilibrium. A septic nipple may have first inclined me to this exploration.

After some fifteen days both breasts ran dry and the good nurse announced, 'Now thank God, you'll have to bottle feed him!' As if identified with Mother's aversion, I declined this form of nourishment, went into a coma, and lost almost half my weight. What inaudible summons brought me back to life, I am as yet unaware. But the return was dramatic. I opened my eyes, drew several deep breaths, grasped the bottle as if my life depended on it (which indeed it did) and began to suck vigorously.

I have never really let go of the thing since. Far be it from me to expatiate on the miseries and pleasures of drink. But my knowledge of this early experience does not depend on hearsay, or a Freudian textbook. It is more dearly acquired and the means by which I won free of the appalling alcoholic blackouts of my early twenties – they were a repetition of that traumatic weaning – let me achieve some self-direction and insight.

Adelaide's conception of child-care was responsible for her choice of baby clothes. From great Aunt Harriet she had inherited some museum pieces. Stiff with embroidery and a good seven feet long they might have done little harm in the first few weeks of childhood. After that they were straitjackets and lethal. Nurse Cowlieshore repeated, 'If you don't put that child in shortenings he'll go off his head.'

Mother ignored her pleas and kept me in the things for a good six months. No doubt it was Mother's fear of vitality which made her insist on such restrictive clothing at a time when her son needed to kick, wave and wriggle to express the joy of being alive – and the fury. Certainly her ideal baby might have resembled one of those large grubs, white and inert, which are found at the roots of a dock-plant. An occasional coo or smile was in order, but for the most part a good child should sleep, feed and be still. Those storms of crying, by which it must relieve its small overcharged being of a zest and rage which in the first months can achieve no other outlet, filled Mother with acute anxiety. Even in later years, she was disturbed as I bounced my own daughter, Julia, on her mattress: a bedtime ritual which for a year or two never staled.

'Thomas, you are over-exciting the child, she'll never sleep!' The sound sleep which usually followed these antics had no effect on Mother's conviction which like Father's obsessions could weather all contradictory evidence.

With so many of her Victorian generation, Adelaide believed that a baby should be born with the innocence of a cherub and the moral rectitude of an Anglican Bishop. Imagination boggles at the projection of such qualities on to so amoral a creature as a baby. However it followed from her delusion that 'temper tantrums' were not the inevitable protest of a child against the frustrations of living, but *contra-natura*. Father localized evil in the colour of human skin and announced towards the end of his life that if scientists stopped messing about with bombs and sputniks and invented some serum which could bring whiteness to black and khaki then the troubles of the world would be over. Mother saw evil in any manifestation of strong feeling. Children must be gentled down as briskly as possible. In later life she would sometimes tell me with quiet pride that unlike other children I was never bad tempered. Only her remarkable ability to be unaware of what she found uncongenial could have led her to this conclusion since I am and always have been irritable and physically violent. Not that by tears, entreaty, threats of the withdrawal of her love, or the punishment of Eliel she did not persuade me to bottle up my savage temper and, incidentally, sow the seeds of those outbreaks of blind violence which in later life have been a trial to those near me.

'That's not my Tommy,' she would sigh damply after some nasty tantrum. 'That's not my darling boy!'

I was not in a position to ask who else it could have been since my teeth had certainly drawn blood from the arm of sister Sylvia, my shoe given a shrewd hack to Nanny's shin. If Eliel had asked this question, and with some tolerance for the self-assertive temper of his bewildered son, then I might have come to terms with my own aggression. I appeared to him, however, more as a rival than a small boy. Up he would leap after some expression of resentment, and I remember with photographic clarity our wild chases round tables and chairs. The outcome was always the same: I would be lugged, kicking and roaring into his study, and there, under two prints of Jesus by some lugubrious German, Eliel would lam into me with the weighty strop with which he administered justice and sharpened his razor.

Such episodes convinced me that Father and I had little in common. Mother, though she had scant sympathy for my self-assertion, did at least give me some value. 'Charm' mattered, and she would be genuinely delighted if complimented by some member of the Mothers' Union or Band of Hope on the quality of my manners, smile or profile. Since it did give me some value I plugged this role of 'Fauntleroy' with all I'd got. In somewhat later years I even enhanced the ambiguous picture by discreet applications of rouge and powder. If Adelaide had been as sympathetic to my imaginative and artistic outgoings as she was to the quiet negative quality of 'charm', then I might have acquiesced to the self-emasculation of homosexuality. Luckily she was not and the dubious crown of inversion was snatched from me.

There were compensations for the surrender (pretended; my penis remained, albeit a secret weapon) of masculinity, which Mother demanded. Intimate forgiving clinches, for instance, after some nasty scene. Our bodies entwined, our faces sharing the moisture of tears, I would hear her croon,

> 'Thorn for the camel
> Fodder for the kine,
> But mother's heart for sleepy head,
> O little son of mine.'

The fact that I was not in the least sleepy, but full of the most interesting sensations did not lessen my zest for these 'huddles' – nor Eliel's anger when he surprised his wife and son in such a hammer-lock. They convinced him of my need for reformation. I have mentioned the bleaching ritual. There were many others. Cheek-drill, for instance. Under his guidance I would puff out my sallow cheeks and slap them vigorously. The object was to gain that English pink which was the outward and visible sign of an inward grace. A receding chin gave proof of weakness and Eliel was convinced that mine receded. Luckily King Alfonso of Spain had found a remedy and under father's guidance I would press jaw to fist, and fist to jaw, relax and press, relax and press . . . relax!

Eliel was also gaining strength at this time, not to mention spiritual comfort, from a nice bit of scientific flummery which was supplied for five guineas post-free by the Swiss firm of Telemou. Seated on his bed and with an expression on his face that was both devout and cloacal, he would grip the two terminals which connected him to a large electric battery and receive 'animal magnetism'. Since the batteries ran down quickly and were somewhat expensive, only when looking exceptionally debilitated was I allowed to be recharged.

More memorable than the slight tingling of Herr Telemou's invention were the lessons which Eliel gave me in shaking hands. Not only the pressure of the grip, but the exact quality of one's gaze at the person greeted were indicative of 'character'. Mine was bad, but at least I could do something about my handshake and not give myself away at a first meeting.

'My boy,' Eliel would announce, 'come into the study for a moment. Now you realize the Bishop will be staying with us over the weekend?'

'Yes, Daddy.'

'He's a good man, a strong man, an excellent judge of character. I want him to think well of you.'

'Yes, Daddy.'

'It's a question of family pride of . . . *noblesse oblige*: so you must learn to shake hands properly. It's surprising what people can learn from a handshake. Now, let's try. Come on, head up, look me in the eyes, put your hand out, grip firmly.'

Nervously I would place my hand in his. The result was far from reassuring.

'No, no, no, Tommy. How can people trust you if you shake hands like that. Slimy, weak . . . slimy! Now, this is the way to do it. Firm, you see, and I look into your eyes, straightforward but without cheek. Try again – and no slyness!'

On and on it would go, my hand getting clammier and clammier, my gaze even more shifty. One day, I spun round, leapt into a leather chair and screaming, 'No, no, no . . .' battered its cushions with my fists. I battered Eliel too, but though my protest did end this particular antic, its immediate result was, as usual, the study and the strop.

Although his discipline was paranoid, in his tortuous mind Father did believe it was for my well-being. That I know from my middle-aged standpoint and knowledge implies forgiveness. At the time, though, if provided with a suitable weapon and the ability to release one or two inhibitions like a safety-catch, I'd have blown his head off before you could say 'Rural Dean'.

My most effective protest against his régime was not on behalf of myself but a large white rat. Although father was by no means a 'Squarson' and would never have 'ridden to hounds', he did believe in blood sports and patronize local meets and the gentry. It was part of the English tradition. One April morning a village bank manager brought his two fox-terriers to the vicarage, and a large white rat. We were to have some sport and I was brought from the nursery to enjoy it. The white strip of life twisted and twirled in its wire cage, pink-eyed and terrified. When it was released on the lawn and after a squeak or two and some seconds of frantic doubling was nipped out of life by a neat dog, my reaction was by no means sporting. I rushed into the kitchen, armed myself with a poker and lammed into Eliel with all I'd got.

Such open revolt was exceptional. For the most part, I swallowed back my fury. It was not infrequently set off by sister Sylvia. In his own somewhat specialized way, Eliel was devoted to this girl who was two years my senior. The desire to love and be loved by a father is innate. Certainly I was jealous of Eliel's demonstrative affection for Sylvia, and assuming she had gained what I longed for because she was a girl, proceeded to make up to him as 'girlishly' as possible. Luckily my simpering and wriggling met not only with indifference but hostility and derision.

But for that I might well be treating purchasable mariners to pints of bitter ale and making tours of the 'cottages'. One has, as Mother would often remark, much to be thankful for!

Like his wife, Eliel had a remarkable blindness to the real needs and nature of young children. Oblivious of the fact that a young child has few ways of self-expression other than a good 'yowl', he chanted his educational theme song: 'Sylvia must never cry!'

Since his study was conveniently placed almost underneath the nursery, at the least sound of protest he would canter upstairs to protect his darling. My shrewd sister took full advantage of the protective umbrella and subjected our various nurses and maids to a Draconian régime. Few could stand the strain. Before the arrival of the redoubtable Miss Naylor who seemed to be posi-tively recharged by the electrical atmosphere of the vicarage, eight nurses gave notice in a period of three years.

Since they feel towards them more as children than husbands, mother-fixated men must have considerable difficulty with their wives whom they regard either as tyrannical police-women, or a curious blend of helot and ever-open milkbar. With a daughter, in part because the relationship is not complicated by overt sexu-ality, they can indulge in an idyll which though dubious does give temporary satisfaction to both parties. Unfortunately the romance in which my father played St. George to Sylvia's fairy princess required a dragon. Once at fighting age, and involved in quarrels with my sister, I was cast for the role. With one ear cocked and his lance within easy reach, Saint George would be under the nursery floor – sermonizing.

'I, like you, my dear brothers and sisters, am a mere man! I, like you, have my cross to bear and a cross can be all the heavier when it concerns our own home.'

It was perfectly safe provided he kept it up. While he was busy demolishing the free-thinker of explaining to the wealthier members of the congregation that 'the eye of a needle' was quite a large gate in the walls of Damascus, and even the plumpest camel could get through with a slight squeeze, then I could get in a telling blow at Sylvia and her secret weapon would be ineffective. Her 'secret weapon' was an enormous bellow and if it came at a pause in the sermonizing then there was hell to pay. With a clatter of hoofs, Saint George would gallop upstairs to the nursery – to find, in point of fact, neither princess nor dragon, only two hot and extremely cross children.

Sometimes Adelaide would intervene; but she lacked confidence in those earlier days and her efforts met with scant success.

'Leave the child alone,' she would plead, 'leave him alone, dear, he meant no harm!'

But Eliel, his blood up and a really unpleasant glint in his eye, saw nothing that resembled a child.

'Stop hiding behind your mother's skirts,' he would bellow, 'come out, be a man!'

And then he would pounce. Round the table I would dodge, out of the door and upstairs, Saint George thudding behind me. But whether I went to earth under a bed or behind some curtains, the end was always the same.

I was terrified; as much by my own fury as of that of Eliel, and for many years could remember few details of those 'wild hunts', the flailing limbs in the study, the gasps and blows, while Adelaide's fists beat upon a locked door. The images would blur as if smudged over by a cloth soaked in redness. However, it was about this time, at the age of six or seven, that I began to catch with my inward ear, far above me in the embattled sky, the tumult of giants fighting. Their wordless thunder would bounce from hill to hill. No doubt this was an intimation of psychic disorder. It was my own outlawed and intolerable fury I heard beyond me. But what is one's own? Does one have, as a personal attribute and possession even the power to lift a hand or raise an eyebrow? What I heard was real enough, and it was the giants exulting in a combat which was also a ceremony of friendship. I think I promised myself that one day I would bring down to earth some fragment of that energy and give it human speech. That was one aspect of my situation. The other was a sense of grief and enclosed anger so overpowering that for many years any casual affront would drive me into a pandemonium of red mist from which there seemed no escape but an act of extreme violence.

# Chapter Four

When I was five the black dreams came;
Nothing after was quite the same.

*Come back early or never come.*

The dark was talking to the dead
The lamp was dark beside my bed.

*Come back early or never come.*

LOUIS MACNEICE

At an early age I believed I had a sensitive understanding of Mother, her water-colours, for instance, her violin and piano playing, far beyond Father. However, our very special understanding was continually and most rudely shaken. Despite his obvious 'unworthiness' Mother would insist on taking his part. I had 'rumbled' him and my ability to pinprick the various masks and pretensions with which he covered his unease caused many explosions.

'Poor old General Bacon,' he would announce at supper after an evening with the parish council of which this ancient warhorse was a member. 'Had to put him in his place today.'

'I hope you weren't too rough, dear,' Adelaide chirruped.

'He suggested we should have special vestments for the choir at Easter. "General," I said, "when you were in the army, you commanded it, but I am in command here." Must say the old fellow is a sport. Took me aside afterwards and said, "Padre, you are a man, I can respect you."'

'Daddy.'

'Yes, my boy.'

'Why did the General say you were a can?'

'A man, Tommy, a man, do listen when your father is speaking.'

'But, Daddy, what else could the General think you are. Surely you must be a man.' I believe I got away with this on the grounds of invincible stupidity. On other occasions I was not so lucky but could never resist this form of father-baiting. Unfortunately Mother could never see the justice of my sallies. 'How dare you speak to your father like that,' she would murmur with the half-closed eyes of a *mater-dolorosa* after some extremely effective quip. 'How dare you!'

At such moments I felt she could give Judas a run for his money and could never understand how a woman of such apparent charm and intelligence could possess such depraved tastes. My 'Oedipal' was developing briskly.

It was particularly strong at bedtime. From fear of the darkness and from a desire to get Mother upstairs and away from 'my rival' in the drawing-room, I would bawl lustily. If she came, and before sitting down on my bed, stood framed in the doorway complete with amber beads, velvet dress, and high crown of red hair, that was a real triumph. There would be more cuddles and assurances of mutual adoration. Also one bit of mother-craft rather more puzzling: although more than five years old and quite capable of performing the operation myself, I would repeatedly desire to urinate, and my mother would hold my penis during the operation between her fingers. Her ostensible object was to direct my urine into the chamber pot, but Eliel, poor soul, was distinctly puzzled when he caught us at this little *folie à deux*. Sexual repression can permit of some interesting variations.

All too often it was Eliel who came galloping upstairs; my heart sank when his short sturdy body loomed into view.

'Go away, I want Mummy.'

'Your mother is having her dinner. Really, Tommy, at times you make me sick! She's been on her feet all day . . .'

'I want Mummy.'

'Self, self, self. Have you no consideration. She's tired, I tell you.'

'I want Mummy.'

'Mummy, Mummy, Mummy. Now try and show me that you have got some spunk and are not a milk-sop. Turn over on your side like a good boy and go to sleep.'

On rare occasions and with no little relief I would follow his advice. But it seemed like selling the pass, and being a boy of principle I preferred to do battle. At times she would come up and that was a win for me, at times he kept her battened down below hatches. But the result of this war was always the same: worn out with tears and emotion I would fall asleep.

Asleep but not at peace. Between the age of five and ten I entered a realm of dreams so vivid and infernal that it overshadowed my waking life and made it difficult to believe in the reality of the daytime world. My energies, largely withdrawn from an environment both restrictive and hostile, were directed to the inner world. I could find no real *modus vivendi* for hatred and love with either of my parents and so turned them towards that twilight dominion which is symbolized in myth and fairy story by subterranean maze, cavern, the country at the back of the North Wind. So silent and withdrawn did I become during these years that both my parents believed I was dwindling to idiocy. Their opinion was shared by Buchanan, the family doctor, a singularly unimaginative Scotsman whose daughter matriculated with unusual distinction – then cut her throat.

For some years I lived in that shadowy no-man's-land which, if you find your way out of it, is the birthplace of myth, poetry, legend, symbol, but whose permanent residents are insane. It is the abode of the talking carp and the wise old woman, the White Goddess, the Minotaur, Medusa, all those creatures who body forth imaginative truth. But since I had been conditioned to fear my own energies, the creatures I met at the back of the North Wind were, for the most part, infernal.

By day as the rooks cawed and the ponies rolled and browsed in their paddock, I would try to forget the horror of darkness I must enter at bed-time. Darkness always came. Then the chairs of the night-nursery, the bookcase, even the Beatrix Potter frieze with its comfortable hedgehogs and rabbits would grow out and away from themselves, I would press my nails into my flesh and blink myself awake but as the darkness thickened and the little flickering night-light took over, then the room became alive with trolls, witches, werewolves, vampires. These last were a particular nuisance after I had read Bram Stoker's *Dracula*, and would flap and scrabble night-long at my bedroom window. Luckily, I got hold of what I imagined to be garlic and they were unable to get into the bedroom. Of course it was my own subjective horrors that shaped themselves out on the screen of darkness. But a fantasy is no less real and independent for being one's own than is a child. And when dissociation begins who knows what alien ghosts may prowl through the unconscious. Jack the Ripper, for instance, I expect his distinguished shade would have found one of my morning fantasies of interest – if he did not inspire it. There is a red room. From its ceiling a number of women (all of them resembling Adelaide) dangle from meat hooks which pierce their nostrils. Their heads are shaved, and with a long thin knife of exceptional keenness I carve rashers of flesh from their living bodies.

In the light of that fantasy (not that at the time there was much light on it) it is not remarkable that my bedtime rituals expressed concern for Mother's welfare.

'You won't die, Mother. Promise you won't die?'

'No, darling,' she murmured with as little insight into the unconscious as an oat cake but flattered by my concern for her welfare. 'Of course Mummy won't die.'

This ritual of exorcism might continue for thirty minutes or an hour. It seemed necessary, but I recall that in the very thick of it some essence of myself stood – detached as a well-breeched Victorian mountaineer on some remote Alp – yawning with boredom.

I had also to be reassured of the bedroom.

'There are no beasts in the room, are there, Mummy?'

'Of course not, darling.'

'Please look.'

She would too, under the bed, behind the curtains, in the wardrobe, and in such a brisk businesslike way it was difficult not to believe in the reality of my ghosts. She wouldn't have looked so diligently if there wasn't a distinct possibility of something being there. And once I tipped over into sleep, there most certainly was. In boots of lead I was pursued up greased, shifting stairways by fanged women. Giants, blind and idiotic, could scent me despite such handicaps, and their great footsteps came nearer and nearer as I floundered knee-deep in a desert of powdered glass. At the moment an enormous six-fingered hand stretched out to grip me, I woke screaming.

'You mustn't worry,' Nanny or Mother would say. 'Nobody ever dreams the same dream twice.'

But I had only to nod off and there the creature was, eyeless, smiling, and fingering an extremely large and nasty cleaver. They were serials, these dreams which bodied out my inner fears and furies. Giants were their theme for a week or two, then witches, vampires, rats. They swarmed in a mesh of fur over the carpet, up the bedclothes and covered me with a sinuous web of rat life. I shudder now, not at those poor rats, but the fear I must have felt for my own energy. We are an image-making creature and the image twisted into life as I felt a hard furry body move in sleep against my footsole. Even broad waking I would be too frightened to stretch out my legs in bed. There was a hard knot of rodent down there. Mother or Nurse would pull back the sheets to reassure me. But I did not believe the empty white linen they showed was untenanted. It only proved that rats were cunning. The unconscious had taken over in those days. I was near to a psychosis from which there might have been no return.

There were eels too. An elder and admired boy took me up a tributary of the Tyne called, appropriately enough, the Devil's Water. My task was to move some large flat stones very gently aside while with eel spear poised my friend waited. From the dithering grains of the moorland stream a slim shape twitched and arrowed. Down came the spear to be raised with an eel writhing on its three prongs. If someone had mentioned the mystery of these creatures, their pilgrimage over corn-stubble and roadway, through drains, ditches and the oiled hiatus of canals to their all-mothering haven in the Atlantic Sargasso, then I might have associated the life in them with my own pilgrimage and not made of them an image that was both alien and destructive. As it was, for many nights I was haunted by their writhing (even beheaded they were unwilling to die) and their cold dry bodies twisted across my flesh in nightmare.

From such vivid dreams I understood how real is the subjective world. Terror, the sense of my humanity breaking into innumerable fragments, was a reasonable price for the conviction I gained in those days of being involved in a dimension of being, which though independent of space and time was no less real than my waking experience. In later life this conviction has been strengthened by moments of imaginative and mystical insight, those telepathic or precognitive happenings which we attempt to exorcize by such clichés as 'coincidence', 'intuition', 'instinct'. Mind you, there is some point in being 'rational'. If the fantasies of the unconscious mind, devoid – this is the meaning of 'unconscious' – of insight or understanding, should coalesce with experiences which though irrational are indubitably true, then our dearly acquired 'sense of reality' would be in hazard. Perhaps this is why I had no immediate, dramatic and, if one equates the word with 'inexplicable', 'supernatural' experience until I was fifty. To quote an authority 'I have many things to say unto you, howbeit you cannot bear them now.' In the August of my fiftieth year the Supernatural both stated itself and was bearable.

For a number of years we had stayed with relations of my wife who owned a villa near Belluno, a small town at the foot of the Italian Dolomites. They lent us three or four of the many rooms of their San Lorenzo. One warm night, whether from catarrh or alcohol, I snored steadily and Margaret took refuge in the divan bed of the library. Not for long though. At 2 a.m. she shook me awake with, 'Thomas, Thomas, come quickly, quick, come and listen!' I followed her to the library. By the wall facing us there was a heavy walnut writing desk. On the flat top of the desk there was an eighteenth-century porcelain figurine of a horse and rider; above and behind, the oil-painting of a Franciscan ancestor whose expression, although my wife insists it is benevolent, I have always thought both hostile and sly.

But the desk was causing trouble. Left, right, centre, from every quarter the raps came; insistent, staccato. There are earth movements in the Dolomites. I placed my hands on the floor and the flat top of the desk – nothing. I opened each drawer for the reassurance of some small animal. They were empty. Then the raps stopped but before our eyes the porcelain horse began to gallop. Up and down it pranced on its base of china. I placed one hand on either side of the figurine; the desk was still, the china horse continued to prance. But, 'If you have anything to say, rap twice!'

those words, delivered in my best pedagogic manner did quench all sound and movement. Although for many years I had believed in the possibility of some inexplicable and dramatic phenomenon intruding into a world that seems both prosaic and determined, this was my first personal experience of such an intrusion. I still find it infinitely reassuring. It would not have been reassuring some forty years earlier when without meaning or insight I wrestled with my private terrors.

There were toads and weasels but my especial monster was a musquash coat and a mask of painted cardboard. It was the evening of my sixth birthday and to celebrate the occasion Sylvia and I were taken to a performance of 'Beauty and the Beast' at the Church Hall. It was given by the Girls' Friendly Society and what actually shuffled on to the stage was a girl in a fur coat, slippers, and a crudely painted animal mask. But all I feared and had thrust under the floors of the mind took shape in that apparition. It touched the spring, the panel glided open and there stood the horror.

'What rash man,' it demanded of a buxom farmer's daughter in breeches and feather cap, 'what rash man has dared to pluck a rose from my garden?'

I walked back to the vicarage my hand glued to Mother's but, unfortunately, speechless with revelation. Darkness had been made visible and now dwelt among us. It was diabolic and omnipotent. A projection, of course, on to a coat and sixpenny mask. But it is remarkable how a projection of some phantom of the mind can be confirmed, not only by meeting similar projections or counter-projections in other people, but by some correspondence in the physical world, a smear of red paint on a wall, a woman who barks like a dog as she passes, a clawed bird twitching in the gutter. Since the night of the play was cold, Mother spread over my sleeping body just that musquash coat which had clothed the Beast. I woke from a dream of the creature, stretched out my hand and touched its pelt. That did it, the fiend was obviously loose. It was not confined to the thickets of nightmare and for many weeks it was my shadow.

Until I was ten years old, my liaison with the Beast and other monsters was, whether asleep or waking, of extreme intimacy. After that age I started to project 'the furies' on to teachers and other school children and box my own shadows in the outer world. In the earlier years, my life had little relationship with other people except my sister and parents. It varied between light and darkness. The same power which in the dusk could invest a towel horse with infernal menace could, when morning came, yield to every bird and tree the glories of paradise. In his books about mescalin, a drug whose dangers he was not aware of, Aldous Huxley has suggested that such a vision may correspond both to ourselves and our environment. However, unable to bear its intensity, an intensity which would not help us with the business of living we filter away great swathes of experience. Certainly Huxley's ideas are supported by many poets and remind me of the open vision of my early years when I divided my time between a celestial and an infernal world.

There was a paddock under my bedroom window in which a cob and pony were kept and Rhode Island Red and Leghorn fowls pecked and crowed and chased each other. Its western corner was overshadowed by a great sycamore tree. Almost every morning its innumerable branches would hold like an offering to the rinsed sky a chattering parliament of rooks. That in later years I picked off a number of these birds with my .22 does not alter the assurance they made of the energies of life. From the tree, the silent upthrust of its being, as it drew life from earth and sky and rain, I gained a similar assurance. I set this sycamore against the terrors of night. It was out there plunging through the darkness and the darkness was made tolerable since I knew the tree could ride out the extremities of storm and continue to be itself though drenched with rain, blacked out with mist and silence.

My father's cronies were less reassuring. As Rural Dean he had numerous visitors. But I am unsure whether the Church of England clerics were at that time and in that place a remarkably odd bunch or whether the oddities were drawn to the Canon. There was Collinson, for instance, who was 'done for' by a disreputable and crapulous sailor he called the 'Bo'sun'. He had an allergy to the female sex more usually associated with cats. This handicap – it could cause a mild rash and panic – made his clerical duties difficult to carry out; but Eliel was sympathetic. Canon Dean was also a frequent if somewhat unwelcome visitor. Long, damp, trembling, but with eyes that were most certainly seeing things not visible to the rank and file of humanity, he would disentangle himself from his ancient Ford.

'There you are, Canon, nice to find you in. One gets lonely in one's little parish, and I always enjoy a good long crack with an intelligent man of the world like yourself.'

Despite the compliment, Eliel had endured a great many of Dean's 'long cracks' and looked extremely uneasy. The incumbent of Sarne brushed aside all excuses. 'No, no, my dear boy, you are, if I may say so, as Rural Dean, my spiritual pastor and master and it's your advice I'm after. They have become exceedingly difficult of late.' 'They' were the evil spirits who gave poor Dean a great deal of trouble. 'The Boys' Brigade has dropped, dropped sadly. The Mothers' Union, why our numbers were down to four at the last meeting! They are working against me.' Father did try to suggest that if his sermons dealt of other things than the whiles of the innumerable devils with whom he was on intimate terms, then more of the stolid yeomen of his parish would attend the church. But Dean knew better.

'No, no, my boy,' he announced looking very suspiciously at a small rose bush. 'I have both seen them with my own eyes and felt them – to my cost! Look at this.'

He drew up the black cloth of a clerical trouser leg and revealed a nasty bruise.

'Their doing. Only last night, my dear wife will bear witness, I was flung violently out of bed by a hostile spirit.'

By no means hostile but deeply interested, I would follow them round the paths of the garden. When Dean got on to his second obsession – it was alchemy – his voice sank to a low murmur.

'I am almost there, my friend, they do all they can to hinder the work, but I persevere. Gold, dear Canon, pure gold, then the Mother-Church will appreciate me.'

This was too much for Eliel and he led his rapt visitor into the house for tea and cucumber sandwiches. Another frequent visitor, and one of whom Eliel seemed genuinely fond, was the Reverend

Peter Coles. 'A saint, my boy, if ever there was one.' Coles was enormously fat with a strangely high-pitched voice. His thin, grey wife bore witness to the price of sanctity by a nervous twitch and a tendency to migraine if any mention was made of sex. Troubled by masturbation as a youth, Coles put his self-control to the test by refusing to consummate his marriage for two years. That the result of their somewhat belated union went 'to the dogs' and the colonies proved only the ingratitude of children.

There was also an ex-headmaster who took holy orders in later life. As a cleric, he had a keen eye for any signs of Romanism; as a headmaster, he was equally watchful for masturbation. 'I can tell, Canon, I used to watch my boys at play and work. A certain slackness, a certain listlessness and that boy does it, that boy is guilty.'

Some three years after we came to Corbridge, a gentleman for whom I did have real affection paid us daily visits. It was discovered that the vicarage was infested with rats and Mr. Armitage was the local rat-catcher. He was broad, bewhiskered and kindly and arrived with three terriers and a large sack. For two engrossing weeks I followed him everywhere as with water, carbide, tar, broken glass, and an assortment of poisons he made stealthy war on the powers of darkness. Looking at his calm face I felt no doubt of the issue of this conflict. Even when he held up a large wire trap of screeching rats and with the statement, 'Strange, Master Tom, you can't give life, but you can take it,' plunged them into a water butt, I knew he was making an affirmation of life. When he left I embraced him with fervour and tears to the embarrassment of Eliel, who considered such expressions of feeling both foreign and effeminate.

# Chapter Five

*Inter urinam et faecem nascimur*     St. Augustine

Up to the age of seven I would frequently sleep in Mother's bed. I did not oust Father from this privileged position since after the first few weeks of marriage he had retired to a separate bedroom. Adelaide snored and a hard-working cleric must have proper rest; moreover whereas she could not sleep without a curtain drawn aside and a window open, he favoured a sealed and tomblike blackness. So for some years I was at times her bedfellow. One thing puzzled me. Should my hands stray between my thighs Mother would announce, 'No, dear, don't ever touch yourself down there, or you won't grow.' Her warning aroused no guilt, only misgivings about the correct method of urinating, and surprise that growth could be checked by touching some part of the body as by the press of a button. But both my parents possessed an unusually well-stocked armour of those guilts and taboos which overshadow sexuality and were biding their time.

Their suspicion of Eros was, in part, a legacy from their parents. Mind you, though in middle age Mother assured me with complete confidence that the female orgasm was an attribute of loose women, and no decent wife could enjoy the duty of sexual intercourse, in later life she took an unflagging interest in her son's amorous adventures and enjoyed the biographies of Madame de Pompadour and Lady Hamilton.

Father's hatred of Eros was more persistent and more virulent. For the opprobrium with which he loaded this god when capable of doing him honour with an adult body, he was punished in his last years by a senile and obsessive sexuality which was singularly inappropriate to his bed-ridden condition. Perhaps punishment is the wrong word since his erotic fantasies were his constant interest. But for all that in old age those impulses to which he had denied

living room circled his white shaken head like a wreath of sea-
birds, lascivious and screaming. They would settle on anything;
my daughter, Julia, for instance. When she visited her grandfather
in the current garb of a teenager, he gave her a very sharp look and
later pronounced a sepulchral warning.

'My boy, is she going out like that?'

'I presume so, and her friend. Anything wrong?'

'You know very well what's wrong. Don't joke with me.'

I knew very well what was going on in his mind but that was
another question.

'Father, I don't understand. Whatever is the matter?'

His poor, shaking head half raised from the pillow, he attempted
that Torquemada glare which in days gone by had quelled the
bravest.

'Her breasts, are they really like that, are they . . . natural?'

'Well, I haven't actually felt them, but, yes, I presume so.'

'I'm telling you this for her good, for your good, for the good
of all of us and you must tell her, tactfully, mind you, what I'm
going to say.'

'Come on then, let's have it.'

His eyes swivelled to the commode in a far corner as if he could
actually see the event there, very nasty and very, very interesting.
'Men will lust after her and that friend as well. They're going the
right way to get themselves raped.'

On the pier presumably and in broad daylight. But what interested me more than the possibility of there being a right and wrong
way of getting raped was that, lacking the discipline of action, the
fantasies of my bed-ridden father, though no doubt latent for half
a life-time, could proliferate and become his world. I thought with
fear as I listened to his strange compulsive statements that if one
does not harrow some part of the unconscious then at death one
may lapse without the chance of insight into a dream from which
it is not possible to awaken, a jungle from which there is no escape.
Mind you, the Gospel does counter 'Where their worm dieth not
and their fire is not quenched' by the statement that we pass out of
Hell when we have 'paid the last farthing'. Certainly I feel that at
his death Eliel had still a debt to pay to life and suspect that he may

reappear in a number of future editions before he settles down to eternity.

Since they handled and cleaned his bed-ridden flesh, the nurses who attended my father in his last decade and illness made for some startling projections. Unmarried or widowed, since narcissism is blind as Cupid, he assumed they found him infinitely desirable. They would, he informed me, derive pleasure from handling his scrotum during the bedbath. Even when tying his shoes he knew they bent needlessly close to his genitals for the pleasure of smell. For the most part this was fantasy. But – think of the Hitler régime – it is remarkable what a response even the wildest and worst dream will elicit from the passivity of much human nature if projected with sufficient intensity. There was some resistance. Eliel was offended when a nurse wore a mask while attending to him on the commode and forbade her to wear the offending article. Shortly afterwards she gave her notice – one more instance of 'man's ingratitude'.

The penultimate couple who attended his last years were the nucleus of some striking daydreams. Indeed Eliel was speculating on the possibility of a convalescing holiday with Mrs. Gleeson, and in Paris, a few weeks before his death. The very tall and emaciated husband of Mrs. Gleeson, who was buxom and Scottish, suffered from arthritis. His tremulous courtesy convinced Eliel that he was a ruined 'ponce' who had exploited Gladys until she was past the age of active service when he decided to marry her. Equally firm was his belief that on her nights off, when to the best of my knowledge she visited her old father in Bournemouth, she was peddling her faded charms on some street corner. He also 'knew' – mother was dead now – that Gladys intended to liquidate her husband with a stiff dose of poison, so anxious was she to be united to him in matrimony.

I know, of course, that long before these fantasies of my father came into their exotic and abundant fruition, he had been afflicted with Parkinson's disease. But although there were somatic reasons for his losing hold on reality I believe that what emerged, when his mind got out of gear with our everyday world, was no accident, but the result of a life-time of fear and sexual repression.

Of his sexual guilts and fears I had first-hand experience at the age of seven. It was then that he chose to warn me of the perils of masturbation. I had at the time neither masturbated nor experienced a 'wet dream'. However 'forewarned is forearmed' and since in a few months I was to enter my eighth year, a preparatory school and the temptations of the world, Eliel did his duty.

It was during a winter evening walk that he stopped, appropriately enough, for his words were to be important, at the junction of two small lanes. I remember his flat old-fashioned clerical hat, his stick slashing at a clump of nettles, the urgency of his voice. He was going to pass on to me something his father had told him many years ago and for which he had always been deeply grateful.

'My boy, there are certain things you can do: wicked, horrible actions. Do you understand me?'

I hadn't a clue; but that it was a solemn occasion was obvious enough.

'If you touch yourself, handle – in a certain way – your . . . private parts, then do you know what will happen?'

'No, Daddy.'

'My dear, dear, boy, be honest with me, have you done it?'

Unfortunately, I had not the faintest notion of what 'it' referred to.

'I am your father, my only desire is to be of help, but how can I help unless you are completely frank with me, unless you are open. Tommy' – (the Torquemada glare came in here) – 'tell me the truth.'

'Yes, Daddy.'

That 'yes' was all he needed.

'Dear boy, for the sake of your mother, for my sake, who love you, I implore you to give up this terrible habit. It can only end in your ruin.'

He gave me his version of 'the facts of life'.

'Your brain is full of grey matter, a kind of jelly. Touch yourself in that evil way and this jelly will leak down your spine, what doctors call the spinal cord, and go to waste.'

I nodded intelligently, impressed by the scientific touch but wondering just how I would be able to piss in future.

'This, my boy, is what the Bible calls the "sin against the Holy Ghost" and there can be no forgiveness for it . . . no forgiveness since you are tampering with the spirit of God. If you rub yourself down there, then the grey stuff will leak out of your . . . your tail, and you'll go mad.

'I've seen boys,' he continued, warming to the good work, 'boys in France and Mauritius who did this, this wicked thing, did worse things, sucked each other's "teapots", torn from home and carried off to the lunatic asylum screaming. Now you must promise me solemnly that you will never, never do it!'

I'd have promised anything. What I couldn't do was pin him down to a few facts. What was he talking about? I doubt if at the time I had experienced an involuntary night emission; let alone induced one. But for all that I was convinced I was guilty of the unpardonable crime. . . . It was a measure of my wickedness that although I had most certainly done 'it' I had no idea what 'it' was. No wonder I felt myself a marked boy, separated like Cain from my fellows.

The conviction of wickedness that Eliel gave me at the cross-roads hinged on innumerable details of my nurture. If there was not something very wrong indeed with me then why should he have smeared my face with bleaching ointment, made me slap my cheeks, put me through the chin and handshaking drill. Despite bouts of explosive hatred I did believe he was working for my good.

No doubt a difficult childhood may foster poetry but in the immediate sense no one could have been more mistaken.

The outer world against which Eliel had warned me was a small preparatory school in Cumberland. Oak Tree House was run by two sisters, maiden ladies of impeccable rectitude whose educational principles were those of Dean Farrar. I remember waiting nervously in the drawing-room for these redoubtable women. There is an impression of straight backs in straight-backed chairs, of thin greying hair scraped from the skull, high lace collars circling two scrawny throats and, when the elder spoke, a smell of fish.

'We have no need to tell you, Canon Blackburn, how deeply important my sister and I feel religion to be in a boy's education, of the Christian principles of our little community.'

They did though and for a good thirty minutes.

I was surprised to see tears in Mother's eyes when she left me because at the time I had no experience of a long absence. But a prefect was summoned to show me round my new domain and very sympathetic he was to the small boy who trailed behind him. He showed me the boot-room, where cricket bats and footballs were also kept. Its smell of linseed oil and dubbin is still with me since there at frequent intervals I was chastised by the brawny and bearded old pedagogue who was the Wasthwaites' secular arm. Etched in even sharper detail are the water closets. On their pitch-pine walls, I succumbed to my first temptation in the outer world. By no means summed up in the large-eyed soulful little boy who had just said farewell to his mother, I was also a young gnome, compulsive and full of spleen. This creature, and, mark you, on his very first visit, scratched on one of those walls with his new pen-knife, the picture of someone using a lavatory. That my action was prompted by motives of which I was unconscious did not prevent the likeness being in depth and considerable detail, nor my adding my own initials to the handiwork.

There was a very solemn assembly in the school hall next morning. I wriggled like an eel and lied like a trooper, but since only a gardener's boy possessed similar initials and he had been distant and busy all day preparing compost, it was obvious that I had not made an auspicious start to my career beyond the vicarage.

# Chapter Six

Can a man enter a second time into his mother's womb?
*Nicodemus* to *Christ*

That was the beginning of a long series of delinquencies. With a determination that was no less effective for being unconscious, I bodied out in my own behaviour the bad dreams of Adelaide and Eliel. What passed for delinquency at Oak Tree House would have been scarcely noticed in most schools of today, but I became an adept at the exact word and deed which would bring down the wrath of the Wasthwaites. For a few months it was a question of drinking water. Olivia, always one for the hygienic fad, read that mixing food and drink was harmful. My first refusal to keep to this rule led to a reprimand, my second a shaking, on the third occasion I was taken off by Mr. Brown and flogged between the cod-pie and suet pudding. Olivia soon forgot about her fad when the weather grew warmer, but a mild oath was a certainty with these sisters who were devoted to *Eric, The Bishop's Shadow, The Thorny Path*. These books were our compulsory reading on the Sabbath, and of some value since they put most of the Oak Tree pupils off this particularly repulsive caricature of Christianity – and for life. 'Damn', 'hell', even 'blackguard', any one of these words would set off the Wasthwaites, who had a bat-like sensitivity for an oath. I would be marched off to the drawing-room, battered with words that smelt of the Old Testament and fish, then chastised by the bearded Latinist as if his job depended on it – as it probably did.

The six purple ridges he produced on my backside, though admired by the other pupils, were as mysterious as my conduct. Why had I sworn within earshot of a dragon? Why had I drawn a sow under my French composition for the stout Miss Culley and created a human earthquake? I was a mystery to myself but even more so to Eliel.

'Bad for arithmetic,' he announced, reading my first report, 'bad for geography, bad for French, bad for Latin, perhaps you cannot help this: stupidity is not a crime, but bad for conduct – that is inexcusable.'

At the end of the second term, the Misses Wasthwaite summoned Mother and gave her the low-down on my character. I was told to wait in the adjacent boot-room and since they left the drawing-room door open, skulked down the passage and overheard a good deal of their diatribe.

The elder sister waded in first: 'Mrs. Blackburn, I'm afraid we have some home truths to tell you about Tommy – truths which you must find both sad and disturbing.'

'Indeed, Miss Wasthwaite?' said Mother, and there was a sharp, cold edge to her voice; like most of the Fenwicks when pressed she had considerable dignity.

'I regret to tell you that your son, far from doing credit to this school which is the very life of my dear sister and myself, has so far been a deplor . . . an unfortunate influence.'

'Really? You do surprise me. At home Tommy has always been an extremely well-behaved little boy.'

That was quite something. Memories of misdeeds rose before me and, goodness, only last holidays hadn't I capped the lot by clambering on to the roof of the maids' 'outside' lavatory and letting down a rat – very large and very dead – on to the bowed head of a cook with whom I was conducting a vendetta. But Mother was taking a pasting now.

It was sister Anne's turn.

'We do not mind that he has made no contribution at all, no contribution to our sale of work for the Waifs and Strays with the exception of this object which one of the maids found stuffed under a cushion.' She took from the table a small raffia mat which looked like a bird's nest. It had been my assignment for the Waifs' jamboree but I gave up hope of making a presentable article and tried to jettison the horrid thing.

Mother took the small, shaggy object, smiled slightly and announced:

'I was not aware, Miss Wasthwaite, that needlework was on your timetable for the boys.'

Both sisters blushed with rage.

'Mrs. Blackburn,' said Anne, 'I am afraid you entirely miss my point. Certainly needlework is not on our syllabus but we try to develop in our pupils the grace of charity. By making useful objects, mats, chair covers, antimacassars, joinery and poker work the children make their own contribution to other children less fortunate than themselves.'

'Quite so, but may I suggest that in future Tommy devotes his time to joinery rather than needlework.'

Mother walked to the waste-paper basket and with a deep sigh dropped in my mat. She was a woman of character. But the Wasthwaites were on the warpath.

'We are avoiding the main issue. There have been incidents, other incidents, immoral and serious. Incidents whose details, because you are Tommy's mother, I will spare you.'

'Boys will be boys,' Olivia struck up with a grisly twinkle. 'After thirty years' experience who should know better than my sister and I. But there is a lack of openness in your son's . . . I was going to say pranks . . . but that word will not do . . .'

'Bad conduct,' said Anne. 'Bad conduct, an element also, Mrs. Blackburn, to use an ugly word, of "deceit". He is not open with us.'

That was true, I wouldn't have trusted either of them as far as I could spit. But Olivia was wading in now.

'There is something strange, something disturbing about your son, that I have never met in my thirty years' work among boys. It is not only that he refuses to be frank with us, but we feel that he criticizes both ourselves and a number of our colleagues!'

That also I could understand. I was a good mimic in those early days and only yesterday evening had paced back from the bathroom to the dormitory, my sponge bag held before me like a tray, my toothbrush outstretched like a spoon – in imitation of Olivia as she wove from bed to bed administering those revolting spoonfuls of prune jam which were supposed to keep us 'regular'. The utter silence which greeted this performance should have warned me, but it was only when halfway down the room that I saw Olivia silent on a bed, glaring like a Gorgon. She did not mention the incident but had obviously pondered it in her heart.

But Mother was softening up: eyes half-closed, and a few tears glittering on the lashes, she had her *mater dolorosa* look. The harangue droned on. Sweating in the passage, and, incidentally adding eavesdropping to my crimes, I waited the miracle which would change me into a blond prince, Mother into my princess and bride, the Wasthwaites into a brace of warty toads I could dispatch by a couple of smacks with a shoe heel. It did not happen. I was haled briskly into the drawing-room, and dressed down: then Mother and I trailed sadly off to the station.

There were few recriminations. Despite her love, Adelaide could never accept the fact that my bad behaviour, whatever its cause, was an expression of myself. Since it confirmed my tendency to turn away from aggressive but potentially creative energies, her attitude was not a blessing. I was weak, there were many tempters in this wicked world. This could account for my lapses and enable Adelaide to maintain the image of her 'good Tommy'. My arms round her neck, my head resting on her bosom, as the little train rumbled towards Corbridge, any encounter with my proper daemon was postponed – if not indefinitely.

My huddle with Mother was extremely stuffy. But there was virtue in this stuffiness. It meant that in those years there was no deep intimacy between us, that intimacy of which freedom is a condition. If there had been, then her dislike of my aggressiveness might have led to greater disturbance. But she was a Fenwick, devoted to the conception of a family, its paternal head, to most conventions. Until later years she was deeply suspicious of any exploratory thought, or thought which suggested life's tragic and turbulent significance, When I tried to share with her those imaginative explorations which from early years have been as much a function of myself as breathing I would be met with smiles or disapproving silence. Her painting was a skilful gentling down of the milder aspects of Nature. Far from hinting at that Wordsworthian Power which expresses itself through mountains, trees, streams, she would neatly snip some aspect of Nature from its tumultuous 'ground' and present a vignette perfect, decorative – dead. It is true that in the later decades of her life, Adelaide seemed to discard mask after mask of platitude and convention so that my final recollection is of a freed spirit looking towards death with resolution and inquiry. But, 'Does he still do that?' she inquired as at the persistence of a bad habit, when told by my brother that I had stayed up late writing verse when on leave from the Merchant Navy.

During the earlier weeks of a holiday, because Mother, like Everest, was there, would be at the breakfast and supper table, I was able to ignore her. Her presence calmed the dread which came from an unacknowledged hatred of our suffocating relationship. I was comparatively free, and there were long solitary bicycle rides through small lanes glittering with starlight and mystery. A certain separation of the ego from those broad reaches of energy which should sustain it may lead a child to find those energies again through the phenomena of wild nature which are their supreme image. I loved tree climbing and would step delicately upwards to those final most slender branches where one could sway to the hither and thithering wind like a swimmer in a tide race. Above all there was that tributary of the Tyne called the Devil's Water. Alone or accompanied by an old poacher, Ian Vaughan, who taught me to fish and to whom I was devoted, I would spend innumerable hours exploring the quick stone-broken water. Line and gut, the flies which bobbed against the stream's downflow, these related me to a lost world. When a trout leaped and turned under my dipping rod and I worked its plump golden body towards the shallows, it seemed a part of myself that I had captured.

Such outgoings were only permissible because Mother was there, back home, some few miles from me. Although I had been conditioned to fear my own vitality and feel some essential 'wrongness' within the very nucleus of myself, she did save me from a sense of total badness by her partial love. But for self-assertion, for aggression, she had no time at all. Consequently, despite her love, these powers of myself were not accepted by Adelaide. They were evil.

I tried to by-pass this impasse (Mother loves me, but she does not love ME) by a togetherness with the woman like that of the foetus with the womb. This 'participation mystique' made each return to Oak Tree House an expulsion from Eden: a hard birth.

The knowledge that every 'lived' day brought me nearer this outgoing marred every enjoyment. When fishing, ferreting, birds'-nesting, bicycling, swimming, time raced away, telescoped into a single moment of being. Such sports were a betrayal of Mother. In the last weeks of the holidays if I did not shadow Adelaide and sit by her side through a dull infinity of tea-parties when time had virtually come to a full-stop, then I would regret it later in the dark days of Oak Tree House. During those stuffy self-immolations, a teacup in my hand, vicars and their wives discoursing on the weather, I would often hear my giants thundering above me. That their thunder resembled guffaws of derision is not surprising.

When a holiday did end it might have been my morning of execution. In order to maintain a *modus vivendi* with my parents I had projected much of my hatred of their repressive régime out and away from the vicarage. The Misses Wasthwaite and one or two members of their staff were unpleasant enough; invested with my fury they were intolerable. I stored a corner of the hayloft with water and victuals and went into ineffectual retreat. I simulated earache and, fitted out with a leather motor cycling cap and ear-plugs of oiled cotton wool – Dr. Buchanan was thick as teak – endured six weeks of boring absenteeism in Colwyn Bay and Llandudno with Aunt Marion and some cousins. It was terminated when unable to endure the tedium I scaled the Great Ormes Head and Marion was told by a doctor that earcap or not I was in good condition. I also stabbed the calf of my leg with one of Mother's hat-pins, an accessible weapon of those days, and when that gesture proved ineffectual, hid under our piano. Eliel found me there, and unable to haul me from the mahogany legs round which I had coiled like a conger eel, called in reinforcements.

'Well, Cecil,' he said to the driver of the hired car, 'what do you think of this young man? Did you carry on like that when you went to school?'

Cecil's response was a tolerant smile and since I liked him (he would when the two of us were alone 'rev' the family Morris up to a good sixty m.p.h.), I crawled from my refuge and got into the car with Adelaide.

Once decanted from the station into our first-class carriage the party warmed up. It was the last breakfast of a condemned man but what I fed on was not peaches and cream or laced coffee but seventy-five minutes of undiluted embrace. The fields sped past. Northumbrian grit-stone gave way to the red sandstone of East Cumberland, I wept, kissed and plastered myself against Adelaide. She, for her part, responded with an ardour that was both inappropriate and, for a small boy, overwhelming. What finally arrived at school was an infinite number of disparate particles. Under the violence of the day's emotion, I had experienced a form of psychological fission.

As if the swaddling clothes of infancy had become part of myself, even when separated from Adelaide, she was still there, curtailing and distorting every thought and movement. Sport I did enjoy under the friendly encouragement of Mr. Watson, an admirable pedagogue who when sacked from Oak Tree for some triviality, made an excellent marriage and started a rival school which eventually put the older institution out of business. There was also real freedom in books; and I delighted in boxing. Sweat, the smell of hot leather, a whiff of blood and the friendly guidance of our visiting pro, Don McQuillan, these made life worth living. But Mother, Mother! for her I must keep the best of myself. For her sake I wore my shabbiest clothes during term time and would never use the school's maroon tie, only its black alternative. Absent from Adelaide, in those drab days, like the hero and heroine of *Wuthering Heights*, I mourned for my lost soul – but with incestuous undertones. Mourning reached a climax if she failed to send one of her bi-weekly letters. I preserved these documents in my pockets – it was a physical identification – and since she was a dutiful letter writer, bulged out as term progressed like a pregnancy.

Mr. Watson, not understanding, understood, and cast a quizzical eye over my bulges.

'What's wrong with you, Tom, you look as if you were going to have a baby . . . Jettison your rubbish, boy. Throw it overboard.'

As time passed it became necessary to circumvent Adelaide. But she had gathered into herself great sweeps of feeling and for many years what remained had little to do either with hatred or love.

I passed a number of exams, I had a number of seedy passages with whores and shopgirls. I did not feel. Later and after a number of years of analysis there was Paulette, a pretty French girl. She was lively and responsive, the antithesis of my repressed and guilt-ridden mother. But her spontaneity and ecstatic enthusiasm masked a state of manic depression which in later life brought her to the unholy offices of shock treatment and asylums for the insane.

At the start of the Hitler war and some three days after we had begun to live together and share a small flat in Bloomsbury, Paulette came home rather late and with an air of uneasy virtue. She had, she informed me, met a Polish seaman, both sad and lonely, and administered comfort by fellating the gentleman in Green Park.

'Well, that's that, stay here and fuck yourself,' I announced, 'but I'm off,' and I started to pack my suitcase. Some minutes later there was a smell of burning. She had offered her hair to a lighted gasfire. The sight of Paulette in the role of Berenice with crisp curls of snapping flame really did it. I put out the conflagration with a wet towel and decided she must 'really care'. She probably did. But luckily the role of husband to this woman, who, though in many ways good-hearted, would in her depressive period, sit for days on end – mute and silent, in her manic days, urinate in the streets, rip open the flies of bus conductors and have coition with whoever was handy – was taken from me. After running the gamut of Fascism and Communism, Paulette became an ardent Pacifist. My signing on in the Merchant Navy as a coal-trimmer was a betrayal of the cause, and when I returned to London after a first trip of eight weeks I found her flat in a state of confusion and occupied by six bearded objectors. Paulette, thoughtful soul, had left saucers of breadcrumbs for the mice and for me a note saying the cause did matter and she had gone to live in Camden Town with a prominent member of a pacifist organization.

# Chapter Seven

Wer't thou my enemy, O thou my friend
How would'st thou worse, I wonder than thou dost
Defeat, thwart me . . .

GERARD MANLEY HOPKINS

Opposite my iron bed in the largest dormitory was a Scottish boy. On Sundays he wore a kilt instead of the usual Eton jacket and striped trousers and, although a favourite of the Wasthwaites, was my particular friend. Ian was a good scholar. Though I refused to work and vied for bottom place in a lowly form with an unfortunate and much bullied youth, who wet his days with tears and his nights with urine, this did not prevent our relationship being one of mutual respect and understanding. We shared a love of birds and trout fishing and when prep was finished would make flies on a small vice. At Scout camps we would climb trees or wade over the mud flats of the Solway to watch oyster-catchers, snipe and dunlin. Although I was invariably his second in field sports, in boxing we were equally matched and our friendship was cemented by sweat and the occasional nose-bleed as we struggled together under the benevolent eye of our instructor. Imagine my horror when I saw another boy, a particularly unpleasant one, tiptoe towards Ian's bed one winter evening and . . . get into it! Although the creaking and gurgling which came from their shared couch made me boil with rage and anxiety I was not aware of its significance.

The rustling and whispered communion of Ian and Francis touched off disturbing emotions. I tried to bear my own feelings and stop this intimacy by magical rites which were both obsessional and ineffective. Above each of our beds on a small shelf were three sacred objects: a Bible, a photograph of Mother, a hairbrush. I had recourse to the Bible. Night after night, as Ian and

Francis rumbled together like a contented stove, I sat upright in bed holding the good book above me and uttered spells.

'Dear Lord Jesus, Saviour of the world, make them stop it. I will obey you in all things, dear Lord Jesus, but make them stop it. Thou wast crucified to save us from sin, Thou who only art pure in all things, make Francis go back to his bed. If he will not, then O God strike him down . . . now God . . . strike him!'

God didn't lift a finger. Indeed it was often well after midnight before Francis tiptoed back to his own bed. I kept my rituals up well after that though, and they included holding my breath for periods of one hundred seconds and raising the Bible above my head until my arm ached. So worn out did I become from these night operations that the Misses Wasthwaite called in the school doctor. The cod-liver oil he prescribed was less effective than the departure of Francis to a public school and my inheriting his place in Ian's bed. There I spent many happy hours untroubled either by guilt or anxiety although my head lay upon my friend's naked stomach. Or vice versa: but our communion went no further, and we rationalized our satisfaction, by a scientific concern for the noises, marine and inexplicable, which came from our stomachs.

The following term Ian departed for a public school and one important morning, I woke to find my lower sheet damp and sticky with a strange liquid. There was also the memory of some remarkable sensations. Since these emissions continued to occur and damped both my sheet and pyjama trousers, it was impossible to deny some personal responsibility and I wrote to Eliel.

'Dear Daddy,
    Something strange is happening, I think I am leaking, I am very, very worried . . .'

It was a call! Like a good soldier, he leapt into action. By return of post there came a small parcel. It contained a cotton reel, a triangular bandage and a letter.

'My dearest Boy,' (Eliel wrote with unusual feeling for we were really up against it now), 'It has happened, the testing time has

come, but we will fight this thing together. You are suffering – I
mentioned this to you some years ago and forewarned is forearmed – from night losses. Remember what I told you. There
is a fluid. It seeps from your brain, down the spinal cord and
out through your "tail", its repeated loss can, indeed will, cause
madness! However, although this misfortune has happened to
you, you are not causing it yourself – for the love you bear to
myself, to God, to your dear mother, never "touch yourself"
down there. You are not causing these losses yourself and THEY
CAN BE CHECKED. They will occur only if you sleep on your
back. Tie this cotton reel into the centre of the bandage. Tie the
bandage round your waist so that the cotton reel fits firmly into
the small of your back. Should you turn over from your side to
your back while asleep the cotton reel will press against you,
waken you up and the danger will be averted. God is merciful!

As ever your loving father,

C.E.A.B.

Very neat and practical. Though the interpretation and intensity
were his own, my father's conviction has some historical backing.
It is echoed by Shakespeare, whose 'Expense of Spirit in a waste of
shame', may imply a belief that one's mental and spiritual powers
are weakened by sexual activity. Donne also remarks that by
sexual intercourse 'We do delightfully ourselves undo'. The inheri-
tance, perhaps, of celibate priesthood, determined to believe that
whatever means may honour and lead to God, sexual congress is
not among them. That in most spheres of human creativity there
is no least association between continence and creation does not
weaken the conviction that only by turning against the source of
life can we fulfil life's intentions. Eliel's gadget did not work.

I dispatched another letter. The reply was a second box and
directive. The gloves were now off – it was a 'hot war'; though I did
not realize that far from seeking to combat evil, Father had enlisted
me in his incessant combat with life itself. The box contained an
instrument and instructions. The instrument had an outer clip of
thin firm steel whose inner edge was serrated with spiked teeth. It
opened outwards and was rather more than an inch in diameter.

Opposite the opening was a very short metal rod which formed the base of an inner clip of light spring steel.

A remarkable invention. The inner clip was just to keep the thing in place, but if you had an erection then your expanding penis pressed into the sharp teeth of the firm outer clip. You were woken up and an ejaculation was avoided. Though patronized by monastic orders and pugilists who associated continence with ferocity, I threw mine away in a fit of anger and have been unable to obtain another model. A pity since it has some historical interest. But I can still remember those teeth biting me out of an erotic dream, the dog grip and the convulsive wriggle with which I tried to ward off an emission of semen.

Sex won; but it was a drastic battle. Eliel's third line of defence, when Eros had routed both a cotton reel and 'The Instrument', arrived in an even larger parcel. It contained a shoe bag and several large sharp pebbles. They were only samples. I must fill the bag full of similar objects and sleep with it tied to my back. Fortunately, after spending many intolerable nights, I gave up the struggle and began to masturbate. This was preferable to Eliel's regimen. At least I did masturbate and masturbating asserted an independence which though guilt-ridden was nearer to heterosexuality and the reality of myself than a cotton reel, a bag of pebbles or a clip of steel.

# Chapter Eight

His captain's hand on his shoulder smote,
Play up and play the game

SIR HENRY NEWBOLT

Although 'put down' for a major public school in my last year at Oak Tree, Adelaide and Eliel read an article in a Sunday paper. Under the heading of 'The New Sodom' it denounced our major public schools. With some truth, perhaps – but I see no reason to exclude the less illustrious. Certainly, I would have preferred my ration of unnatural vice at one of the 'top ten' rather than the minor institution which my parents quite wrongly imagined was of irreproachable rectitude.

I entered Lanchester at the age of thirteen and being an intolerant, snobbish boy felt that its inmates, sons for the most part of prosperous Midland businessmen, fell far short of my former companions. My comments on their table-manners and accents gave me my first real taste of unpopularity – with other school-boys. It was increased by my denouncing any manifestations of homosexuality – these denunciations were frequent. Although not mentioned in its prospectus, Lanchester had an extremely lively sex life.

Despite the reputed sexual prowess of sailors, not to mention the activities of such prodigies of work as Dickens or Victor Hugo, the English upper and middle classes still cherish the belief that hard work and abundant exercise are more than a match for Eros. I am not in a position to assess the academic standard of Lanchester – it was probably fairly low – but we certainly had plenty of exercise. It did nothing to change the inevitable result of cooping up for months on end and without a scrap of female company, some five hundred boys whose ages ranged from thirteen to nineteen.

There were 'cases'; many members of the upper school had

some junior favourite they would accompany on Sunday walks in the neighbouring woods and to whom they would address letters of endearment. The younger boy would be flattered by the attention of a hero of the 1st XV or XI and do his best to reply with the right fervour. Some particularly fancied youths prinked about the place like favoured 'tarts', took liberties with staff and prefects, and were protected from bullying by their numerous admirers. What happened between the younger boy and his admirer I never discovered at first hand. A dour, prickly boy, suspicious of any one older than myself, I had no 'followers'. My closed embrace was with a fat and fussy prefect to whom – to his extreme dissatisfaction – I had been allotted fag. He expressed his dislike of my brew of cocoa – it was probably nauseating – by flinging the stuff at me. That did it! His cries for help, when I'd got him down and was bumping his head on the floor, soon brought up reinforcements. I was chastised by Mr. Morgan, our long grey housemaster, and allotted to a new slave-driver: Johnson was full-back for the 1st XV and would permit no liberties. I still remember him with nausea.

I expect in the gauche fumble and unbuttoning of things, the school's liaisons went no further than a few kisses and a little mutual masturbation. Like mountaineering, sodomy is a specialized taste and requires a certain expertise. These meetings did something to sweeten the dreary routine of a public school. It can do with it.

Besides woodland grottoes and encounters in the lavatory – a building associated from time immemorial with the sport – there was the Lanchester brothel. We had very large and beautiful playing fields and at their remotest corner, shaded by beech trees and a thicket of laurel, was a large rusty boiler.

I remember the Headmaster showing Mother and me round the school on my first day. 'Quite out of place,' he remarked, 'quite out of place, an old boiler beside this green . . . ah-hum sward and our superb beeches, but you know it has become quite a part of our tradition and the boys – curious creatures, I still find them inscrutable after more than thirty years in the profession – are remarkably fond of it, believe me, remarkably fond.'

They certainly were. It had an opening, well screened by the laurels, that it was just possible to squeeze through. On hot afternoons couples would stroll about waiting for their turn in the boiler of love. Not that I had much success in the thing. On one occasion I did entice a smaller boy inside. But some enhancement of self-esteem was a condition of any junior's response – small boys can give whores a good run for their money. I was too disreputable a character to increase the prestige of my favourite. My opening gambit met with a swift kick, then Warren twitched through the manhole like a lizard. A later attempt was even more unsatisfactory. But I bore no ill-will to the small boy who secured me nine strokes from the housemaster. My approach was closer to rape than seduction.

The ability not to see what we do not wish to see is without limit. The masters of Lanchester – for the most part moral as they come and 'full of high sentence if a bit obtuse' – just did not notice the obvious sexual traffic of the Old School. The only sin was to be caught *in flagrante delicto*. Then the punishment fitted the crime in that the perversion of flagellation struck home against inverted sex. Only on one occasion was a boy expelled. He was discovered kissing an attractive housemaid. Heterosexuality was frowned on.

One very special Sunday, our most distinguished old boy – he was of course a general – came to give the sermon. Chapel was compulsory, once on weekdays, twice on Sunday, but this time it was preceded by a military inspection.

'My dear Blackburn,' the young master gave me a very critical 'once over', 'I assume you do not intend to cut chapel?'

'No, sir, of course not.'

'Are you aware that a distinguished general, an old boy of this school, is going to address it?'

'Yes, sir, couldn't help hearing, heard nothing else for weeks, sir.'

'Spare me your witticisms. General Winters is accustomed to cleanliness and tidiness. He will expect a decent turn out from the members of his old school.'

'Yes, sir.'

'Then, for God's sake, retire, wash, brush your clothes, your hair too, do your tie – decently. Then come and see me again.'

In the end I passed muster and was glad not to have missed the harangue. It was quite something. Although retired for more than a decade, Winters was in full regalia. He did not deliver his sermon from the pulpit – that might have given priority to the Almighty – but from the chancel steps, bang in front of the altar. Nor did he start with any mention of the Trinity or request for grace. 'Fellow soldiers of Christ,' he barked, 'Masters and boys of Lanchester, members of the British Empire.' For twenty minutes we were duly exhorted to chastity, manliness, playing the game, and duty. Then Winters changed gear and his sermon became interesting.

'Up to now, boys, I have talked of the sterner things of life, but these sterner things depend upon someone we all know, someone infinitely tender. When I think of my campaigns, not uncrowned by success, the Somme, Ypres' – (he had played a part in many sanguinary disasters) – 'I am proud, but all the more proud of a little lady, a little lady in grey with silver hair. For it was she, my mother, who inspired me, who spurred me on, who gave me the courage by her devotion "to strive to seek, to find and not to yield".'

There were quite a number of dewy eyes among the older members of the staff and I regret that no one waved us into a rousing cheer for his repulsive sentiments, not unconnected with the death of many thousands. Though his centre was chocolate-cream, the general was lethal.

My new fag-master was a stalwart but sadistic youth. He loved to get me crouched down in a corner and then prod me in the ribs and stomach with a cricket stump. This went on until one evening, ignoring my Caliban-like presence in a corner, he settled down to trigonometry. I bided my time until he was thoroughly immersed, then grasped that cricket stump and gave him a swipe across the mouth. The result was a swollen, lacerated lip – and freedom. True to his creed my mentor attributed the unsporting swipe to an accident in the gymnasium. There was, I concluded, something to be said for the public school spirit.

These schools, like some monastic orders, gather to themselves innumerable formulae and petty restrictions to compensate for their unrelatedness to whatever is signified by 'reality'. Year by year a pupil is relieved of these taboos. Their reduction, though based on no personal merit, only longevity, gives satisfaction to all but those rebels who despise the pettifogging nonsense from the start and, though undesired by the public schools, are the system's principal justification. Perhaps to compensate for her lack of any time-worn tradition or illustrious pupils, Lanchester had a particularly violent rash of these restrictions. They reduced me to despair and fury. They also gave me a dislike of meaningless regulations for which I am grateful. During the first term both trouser pockets must be sewn up. In the second one might be unsewn but you were not, until the third term, and the release of the second pocket, allowed to put your hand in the first. Only in the fourth term were you allowed to slouch about with your hands in both. Prefects and heads of studies kept a sharp eye on these regulations.

There was a large green in the centre of the school buildings with chestnut trees and one very fine mulberry. In the first term you could only walk anti-clockwise around it. In the second term, you could walk clockwise up to the mulberry tree but then must turn about and proceed anti-clockwise. In the third term you could circulate both ways. Though prefects were often concealed behind that tree, and the result of an infringement was three strokes, my chastisements were frequent since I could never memorize or accept these bits of nonsense. Nor could I remember the various boring details by which after two or three weeks new boys were examined by the senior members of the second year. The names of prefects, their athletic achievements, that the emblem of my house was an elm leaf, Allenby's a clover leaf, Smerdon's an oak leaf, try as I might, these details escaped me. Nor, though failure in the examination was often punished by a beating, a hand-traverse round the hot-pipes of our junior common room, and in cases of especial delinquency the coating of the culprit's genitals with boot-blacking, did I suffer these indignities. They were attempted but after one examiner in the ritual of Morgan's house had been kicked in the groin, another bitten in the forearm, I was excused as incorrigible. Not that my resistance achieved any popularity. At the end of the third term, first-year boys were sent out on the ultimate Sunday to gather hickory sticks with which they would be chastised if they failed the final examination. I railed against this imposition, but off I went, with my fellow pupils, to get the rods in. I broke a few but not enough to stop the chastisement of their sycophantic bottoms. After all, it was worth it, next year they themselves would be able to inflict a similar torment upon a fresh crop of new boys.

Johnson, my fag-master, was interesting on religion. He didn't believe in it, and night after night would regale the dormitory he was in charge of with an account of its follies. The Virgin Birth, the Trinity, the Holy Ghost, the Resurrection; he made short work of the lot.

Although there may be periods in which it is latent, I believe now that there is a religious instinct, that it is as imperative as our sexual drives, and in this day and age even more liable to repression. It is concerned with our maturation towards death and if we repress the deathward intention of our lives it will manifest itself in symptoms both innumerable and destructive; the 'ton up' on the motorway, the overstressing of the sadistic components of sexuality, the automatism of unconscious violence, the skull, bones and black leather jackets of the rockers.

Until Johnson got going on my 'faith', it was associated with Eliel. After all there he was in the House of God – performing – the accredited representative of divine power. It is true that my belief in his infallibility had already been shaken. After a sharp row on the vicarage lawn he proclaimed that I would be struck dead by the Almighty, and within thirty seconds. I was the possessor of a new watch – a gift from Aunt Marion – and ticked off the time for blasting. 'Fifty, forty, thirty, twenty, ten – zero!'

Though Eliel looked a trifle crest-fallen when no bolt fell, this incident was removed from everyday experience by the heat of anger. Faith remained; an emotional and intellectual involvement with Christ's incarnation and passion, a delight in various passages of the Gospels, and, unfortunately, a sneaking suspicion that all three persons of the Trinity shared Father's opinions and prejudices. In consequence my attitude to the Almighty was distinctly mixed, and when Johnson delivered his polemic I wrote for reassurance. I would never mention bullying; children assume, usually with some justification, that this is their own fault. Faith was another matter. As a result of my letter Eliel wrote to Morgan who summoned me to his study.

'Blackburn,' Morgan gave a deep sigh – his sole ambition was to slough off his troublesome charges and retire to a cottage in the Cotswolds – 'You have faith, I presume?'

'Yes, sir, I think so, sir.'

'Well then, dear boy, if you have faith, your beliefs cannot be menaced by idle chatter and clever argument. Faith delivers you "from a multitude of opinions", faith is invincible. Good-day, dear boy. I hope I have reassured you.'

I do agree with Morgan, but at that time his remarks were of little help to a teenager subject to the onslaughts of rationalism. I wrote once more to Eliel and his reply blew my phoney orthodoxy to smithereens.

'Dear Tommy,
    You begin to have "doubts". We all go through this. It is a stage. But I enclose part of an article I have just written for the parish magazine. It is irrefutable.'

The passage followed.
    'When the mighty brain of the freethinker which has searched the heavens and sounded the seas has found one spot of ground where a decent man may rear his children in freedom and security and the Cross of Christ has not been there before, it will then be in order for him to air his views.'

This was a revelation. Eliel had not got the answer and was stalling. For many weeks I felt empty and lost. The uncertainty remains. I do not wish to lose it, since my present uncertainty implies a strenuous questioning, and the conviction that although death may be extremely interesting, we are no more in a position to make generalizations about it than is the unborn child of the world he is about to enter. This attitude is closer to the supernatural world than the bogus 'faith' which crumbled away with Eliel's letter. If I had not lost it then a much later experience which confirmed my religious instinct might have lacked living room. During the Hitler War I was invalided from the Merchant Navy with bronchial pneumonia. No antibiotics or M & B were available and for many weeks I would wake up each morning and fight for breath, my lungs choked with mucus, and powdered glass. But on one occasion I woke to find I was not centred in my coughing and retching body. From a far corner of the room, some other 'I' watched with interest but no pain the creature that choked and retched on a steaming bed. That experience first convinced me I was not identified with an everyday self or perdurable body. It has been a constant theme of my verse.

At Lanchester, though, I did 'lose my faith'. Since I was due for confirmation at the time I mentioned my state of mind to Peter Crow, our Chaplain. He looked serious but said nothing. The next day a prefect took me to the headmaster.

Knock, knock. A pause, then faint and preoccupied:

'Come in, will you.' The great man was busy writing a letter and kept me standing there sheepishly for several minutes.

'Well?'

'Blackburn, sir, of Morgan's House, you sent for me.'

'Blackburn . . . ?'

'Yes, sir.'

'Blackburn? Ah yes, Blackburn . . . the chaplain tells me you are a . . . freethinker.'

'Sir . . . I . . .'

'No, don't interrupt my train of thought. Yes, umm. Yes. All I can say is I am very sorry for you. Good-day.'

If I had not got confirmed my name would have been typed alone and scarlet at the foot of the other members of the form who, since it was the 'done thing' at the time, were all confirmees. I determined to take a liberal stand and was duly made a communicating member of the Church of England.

# Chapter Nine

*Ave atque vale*

At the end of my second week at Lanchester I read a notice that all interested in boxing should attend the gym the next evening and sauntered down for a try out. As it begins with 'B' my name soon came round and Sergeant-Major Doran, a pleasant springy little man, had a word with me.

'Going to put you up against a rather bigger fellow, Blackburn, just turns out that way, hope you don't mind.'

I was bored and frustrated and wouldn't have minded anything that promised a bit of excitement. Blagden made a somewhat fancy show with his gloves, but I got under his guard in a few seconds and attacked him with gusto. After three minutes the round ended and my opponent retired from the fight with a nose-bleed.

'What about you now, Waldow?' Doran asked of a second year boy with a broken nose and a certain pugilistic reputation. 'Have a go?' Waldow was demolished and three others before Doran, his eyes sparkling as if he had discovered a promising terrier, reluctantly called a halt. Some months later he found it difficult to understand how a boy who boxed well and could shoot a .303 with some accuracy was quite hopeless at military drill and made such a mess when preparing equipment that he was debarred from O.T.C. inspections. Doran would often regard me with a puzzled expression; the contrariness of human nature!

I became welter-weight champion of Lanchester but it was not only in the boxing ring that I felt possessed. On the Rugby field I also felt myself gathered up and directed by a power greater than my own. In the fourth term I was picked as a forward for the Colts, a sort of junior 1st XV and would tackle, pass and swerve as if during the game the schism was healed between myself and my own 'daemon'. This at-oneness was always preceded by anxiety.

As I waited for the whistle to blow and the long ball sail forward, or the referee to announce 'First round, seconds out of the ring, time', then my mouth went dry, my heart pounded and worms of electricity crept over my stomach. But for some years, once the whistle had been blown, the bell rung, the word uttered, all that dread changed into energy. I left my troubled personal self for an impersonal and single being whose existence was summed up by each moment of combat.

Games made life worth living, but at the age of sixteen, the power left me. Many adolescents, tired with the effort of growing, have a period of lassitude. Mine was increased by Eliel's response to a report of my athletic progress in the Lanchester Magazine. I had been waiting for the Easter number for some days with extreme excitement. Surely it would at last disprove the worthlessness suggested by so many aspects of his 'education'. It was by my plate at breakfast and I tore open the package. Everything was there, welter-weight champion of the school, capped for my house and the 2nd XV, awarded a medal for long-distance swimming. I passed the magazine over to Father – now he must realize I had some value. Eliel regarded the picture of myself with crossed arms and a striped jersey in the 2nd XV, he whisked through the account of my welter-weight victory – 'Blackburn and Clore were both good, but Blackburn's reach and strong left gained him the final'. He looked with increasing distaste at the account of a try I had scored against a well-known Roman Catholic school and closing the magazine without passing it over to Mother, got up from the table and walked towards me.

'Very good, my boy.' He ran his fingers through my short dark hair, raised his hand to his nose and sniffed it.

'Animal, pure animal! You are lucky not to have to think, not to worry.' He sniffed again. 'Pure animal!'

His reaction was conditioned by a personal inferiority for which he suffered all the more deeply because it was unconscious; but it was by no means helpful. Even my athletic skill was but another proof of unworthiness. My self-evaluation was at that time, if not identified, closely interwoven with that of Eliel. I suspect it was his 'pure animal' that caused in part my athletic collapse and a contempt for physical prowess which lasted until at the age of twenty-three I discovered to my salvation and delight the sport of mountaineering.

'What's happened to you?' asked an even more puzzled Doran. 'Very promising you were indeed, very promising, but now – what the devil's happened to you?'

That, as a member of the 'remnants', a scrap heap of footballers who lounged about on the last of all pitches in the thickest possible jerseys, I was not in a position to answer.

Though this rejection of sport may have been inevitable, its result was very bad indeed. Through violent activity I had been able to express in a way that was socially acceptable the violence within me, and so make some adjustment to society. Deprived of this outlet the Furies turned against myself and my neighbour. They became guilt – and delinquency. Without distinction at boxing or football, my role of Ishmael was confirmed. I was disliked by most of the pupils and masters. I dreamt of an existence on some island, inhabited only by birds; I did no work.

With one exception. Mr. Ross suffered from asthma and though an admirable disciplinarian, cared for his disease by speaking as little as possible. When he did speak it was with a loose gurgle which seemed to come from a swamp in the depths of his long body. This admirable teacher had three passions, all of which he communicated to me; his French wife, fly-fishing, Shakespeare.

His wife, a romantic creature, also liked me and noticing on what bad terms I lived with most Lanchestrians, attributed it to the innate dislike of mediocrity for genius.

'Ah, Thomas, *mon cher*,' she would coo over her tea-table to which I was often invited, 'you have it, the divine spark, so heed never those other *garçons, le canaille*. It is Rimbaud, again, my Paul' – this to Ross sucking contentedly at his pipe – 'Rimbaud, Verlaine, Byron, so they must 'ate you. But fight, *mon* Thomas, for the man of genius, *c'est toujours, toujours la guerre!*'

From behind his pipe or tea and sandwich, Ross watched his wife with real appreciation, not for her psychological acumen but the animation of her delightful features. For my part I was both reassured and completely baffled. What did she mean by 'genius', and who on earth were Rimbaud and Byron? I could understand her husband's passion for fly fishing. It determined his teaching 'method'. Year after year his form studied in great detail Izaak Walton's *Compleat Angler*.

Perhaps, since I alone shared his delight in Walton's admirable descriptions of live-baiting, ground-baiting, the 'personality' of a stream in its bends and shallows, the longevity of carp, the inedibility of grayling, he awarded me the middle-school prize for English. It was *Fly Fishing* by Earl Grey of Falloden.

Mr. Ross's third passion was Shakespeare. Because of a certain 'dullness' I remained in his form for two years; as in both of them we studied *Macbeth* I imagine this was his favourite work. An excellent choice; a jolly romp through such boring pieces as *Twelfth Night* or *Henry V* might have postponed my appreciation of Shakespeare for a decade. Not that the 'methods' of Mr. Ross would have endeared him to modern English specialists. We read round the form from right to left, each speech following the position of our desks rather than the demands of drama. No attention was paid to histrionic ability – he would have been horrified at the idea of us coming out and acting the thing. Diction was also ignored and the fact that as a result of his system though engaged in a passionate dialogue, Macbeth might be in one corner of the room, his wife in another. The witches were also dispersed.

Ross cared for none of these things; he did believe in a detailed knowledge of the play but since he wished to relieve his asthma left us to work it out through the notes of Verity, though he himself provided weekly tests. He also favoured 'learning by heart'. It saved his breath and as far as I was concerned proved a delightful exercise though I still remember with impatient embarrassment the desperate grunting delivery of some particularly moving passage by boys who had scant feeling for poetry and in consequence were unable to commit it to memory.

' "Tomorrow and tomorrow and . . ." '

' "Tomorrow," York,' Ross helped him gently on.

' "Creeps in this petty pace from day to day to the last syllabus." '

' "Syllable", York. Syllable means the final word which Macbeth had almost reached at the end of his dark, perplexing journey.

Syllabus refers to a time-table or scheme of work such as you your-self are supposed to be involved with.'

I am glad to say Ross's asthma ceased with middle-age, that he had three children who 'did well', and that he eventually became headmaster of another school. I am also glad that at the end of my time with him I knew *Macbeth* by heart; the tedium of his presentation of the masterpiece was a small price to pay for such knowledge.

Preparation was from seven to eight p.m. and, for the middle school, took place in a long oak-panelled refectory. At times, I would sit at the back and curry favour with the mammon of righteousness by baiting any master who was 'baitable'. There were rounded unspillable inkpots that one could bowl under the desks towards some uncertain newcomer who was making the mistake of trying to be liked by his pupils.

My triumph in this sport was to place a large blob of mixed ink and boot-blacking upon the seat of a nervous young graduate who sported a fashionable light-coloured flannel suit. As he strode up and down the refectory, too anxious to be aware of the malicious glitter in sixty pairs of eyes, I felt for a brief spell that I was indeed 'one of the boys'.

Such behaviour did not fit in with my usual occupation. Indifferent to our stint of parsing, Latin verbs, algebra, in the remotest corner of that vast room, I would compose – not sermons – but expositions as to the nature of God, the relationship of a supposedly omnipotent Deity to a corrupt world, of Christ to our fallen humanity. Such themes are still my preoccupation. It never occurred to me to show these discourses to anyone or collect them in a note-book; indeed, I always destroyed them when the argument was complete. Only once was I nearly discovered. My apparent diligence during prep, but very low form and position, made Robert Curson curious. Luckily I grabbed the papers back before he had time to read more than, 'Christ is the normal man, we are subnormal. Imagine a number of fishes destined to climb out of their muddy pool and become land creatures. Only one fulfils its destiny, that one would be Christ.' The scuffle was over-heard by Mr. Woolaston, the prep master of the day and when told its cause, he looked at me curiously and said, 'Who knows, you may have a poet or future philosopher among you?' His suggestion by no means improved my position and I had many fights with Curson. Also in later life a strange meeting. Though popular with boys, as a young man he was perhaps less successful with the opposite sex and I met him sitting disconsolately in a bar off Piccadilly Circus at a time when the Street Offences Act had not delivered the prostitute over to the mercy of the ponce, created a brisk trade in near beer, and an army of *voyeurs*. Curson wished to be introduced to the delights of women and offered me three pounds to arrange it. Since I knew at least three whores who would oblige for a guinea this was a windfall. We went to the beat of a young woman of Sackville Street, who introduced him to an aged but active relation of hers – also in the game. He found the arrangement satisfactory. Certainly, on the fragments that remained, my friend and I passed a pleasant evening.

At the age of sixteen I discovered poetry. It was Shelley's 'Ode to the West Wind', and as the charged words gathered me into the sweep of their incantation, the experience, a marriage of thought and feeling, although almost unbearable, resolved the schism within myself even more effectively than boxing or football. This was 'being'; while I read the poem I became the poem. Though I felt both joy and terror, from now on poetry existed and was a reason for living.

It never occurred to me that I should mention to teachers or parents the fearful beatitude I gained from Shelley's shorter poems and the odes of John Keats. I am glad of this. The intensity of feeling might have been diluted if I had tried to share it with even the most sympathetic listener. Poetry is poetry. It is not a form of remedial therapy. It made life significant but it did not at that time help me to adjust to society. Far from it; soon after reading Shelley's Ode and as if trying to find outside in the everyday world some equivalent to the excitement produced by the poem, I started to break bounds. It was not difficult. You doubled through some grass at the bottom of the playing fields, round a hedge or two, got up a wall by a thick creeper, down by a few nicks in the stonework and into the street. The obstacles added zest to the glass or two of cider I enjoyed in a small pub. Unfortunately as the weeks went by, these excursions must have blazed quite a trail. One winter evening I dropped down the wall to confront a brace of prefects, complete with boaters, swagger coats and an expression of moral rectitude.

The headmaster was a simple soul; fear made me eloquent, and he really did swallow my impassioned appeal to his sporting instincts. Stalky and Co., Percy F. Westerman, John Buchan, I supported the innocence, the manly adventure of my little prank by the most respectable authorities. He would, he told me, be lenient, and even patted me on the shoulder as I left his study. Unfortunately, by Lanchestrian tradition corporal punishment was only administered by the headmaster at noon on Fridays. My offence had taken place on a Tuesday so for more than two days I brooded. I'd had some fairly savage floggings at the place, four strokes from many prefects, six from masters and on one occasion, nine from my housemaster. It seemed to go on a rising scale, so chastisement from the Head would be quite something. I worked myself into a state of utter panic and when the hour came, despite diarrhoea, presented to Mr. Lake a backside enhanced by gym shorts, two pairs of pants and a large silk handkerchief. This vision was most certainly not in the tradition of Kipling and John Buchan. The Head was not amused. He had been deceived and proved gullible. I was told to remove my trousers, strip down to a thin pair of pants and received fourteen strokes at one bending.

However, Lake's suggestion in my next report that I was making little progress at Lanchester and was unlikely to achieve my goal of Cambridge University was all to the good. In the following term I entered a crammer's.

My later visits to public schools have been to read and discuss my poetry as a guest of modest distinction. They have confirmed my suspicion of these time-honoured anachronisms. By incarcerating boys of such varying degrees of age without female companionship, by isolating masters in a small closed community, the tendency is towards emotional sterility, a divorce of intellect and emotion which may stifle artistic, or indeed any kind of creation.

One English master, whom I had met rock-climbing in the

Llanberis Pass, asked me to explain a poem of mine to his literary society. He had had the piece cyclostyled and circulated and since the boys ranged from thirteen to nineteen and the poem was quite obviously about divorce and adultery I refused either to explain or to read it.

'But why not, old chap, they're all as keen as mustard to hear you.'

'Then they can be as keen as mustard about another poem. This one happens to be about adultery and the breakdown of a marriage.'

His face fell. 'You don't mean it. Goodness me, I thought it was about a mountaineering expedition!'

On another occasion I was confronted by fifty expressionless boys at a school famous for its military associations. At the end of my talk and reading, no questions were forthcoming from those overdisciplined creatures. But Mr. Glazier, the senior English master, stepped into the breach.

'Do you,' he inquired earnestly, 'write more poems in the Spring?'

'Do you imagine that I am a crocus or a sparrow?'

There was a wan titter. But Mr. Glazier was distressed. A fond illusion had gone.

'But I thought poets always wrote more in the Spring,' he murmured sadly.

# Chapter Ten

And Cain said unto the Lord . . . . I shall be a
fugitive and a vagabond in the earth.

*Genesis*

The cramming establishment I entered at the age of seventeen was
a gentlemanly affair. We dressed for dinner on two evenings of
the week and a favourite story of Herbert Weaver, who owned
Ransom Hall, concerned a point of etiquette. Some years previously, through an oversight of the scholastic agency, they had been
sent an assistant from a grammar school. On the first evening of
term, this unfortunate young man appeared for dinner, in an 'off
the peg' dinner-jacket and a bow tie that was obviously 'made up'.
The hush which greeted his appearance turned to laughter when
he blew on his soup.

'My old father dealt with the fellow,' said Herbert; ' "Johnson,"
he roared – Johnson was our butler – "fetch Mr. Rowntree the
bellows from my study, he seems in need of them." '

When I entered the Hall it had somewhat fallen from this
Edwardian 'rectitude'. But my presence and that of another youth,
extremely wealthy, but also from a minor public school, were
compensated by two or three old Etonians and Herbert's wife.
Lady Lavinia was the daughter of a Scottish Earl and may have
been a most pleasant woman. Certainly she gave to her daughters
and poultry an uncramping care and affection, and to us students
was both courteous and friendly. But Herbert had soured her.
Intended, so he told us, for grand opera, some small defect of the
vocal chords had frustrated his destiny. He was an opera star but
reduced by fate to trilling about the house and spirited renderings
of 'Get along, little dogie' in various parish halls. To compensate
for this frustration he seduced whatever was handy.

Lady Lavinia might have tolerated a mistress in London or

even the nearby market town; she found it hard to endure his monotonous seduction of her parlourmaids. I remember one little number; after an up-river excursion in his punt, she returned flushed and rumpled and at dinner treated Herbert with a jovial frivolity which reduced Lavinia to irony, then bitter silence.

I started to drink at Ransom Hall and though my sexual activity was limited to a brief kiss or two on some secluded park bench, enjoyed revelation after revelation as alcohol dissolved the strait-jacket of my self-consciousness. In those days, three or four whiskies put out of action the guilt which may be localized in some particular area of the brain. Drink enabled me to 'see' and 'feel' with that clarity we often associate with childhood. The evening shadows of the streets, the bottles of a saloon bar, the river where we accosted our patrolling girls achieved a dark and glittering majesty which though occasioned by alcohol seemed more real than the data of a sober and unexpanded vision. 'If the doors of perception were cleansed, one would perceive the infinite in all things.'

Unfortunately, drink is an unreliable short-cut to such an enhancement of vision. It did loosen my tongue though, release me from the shyness which would often reduce my conversation to a handful of clumsy platitudes. It enabled me to speak with intelligence and freedom.

At the age of fifteen or sixteen, before discovering alcohol, I would squire my sister to various dances and hunt balls, like an adolescent Prufrock, unable to make one spontaneous remark or unrehearsed movement. There was a particularly splendid affair at Rabey Castle. We joined forces with our cousins, and since there was only one other male in the party and Aunt had insisted that all her four daughters attend including the little mongol, it was a tough assignment. But I shall never forget the young men in pink hunting coats, the ecstatic girls, more remote than angels, with whom under galaxies of candelabra they swung round the dancing floor, gathered up into themselves and with no glint of an eye for the dowagers who waved elaborate fans over their remarkable bosoms, the suits of armour, the paintings of the dead.

Slowly and soberly I waltzed with cousin Lydia, red-faced, panting, speechless. One-two-three, one-two-three, one-two-three, we wove our slow way through a sinuous and whirling Elysium. But I am glad I had not then discovered drink. With alcohol inside me I would undoubtedly have left my sister and cousins, picked up with somebody and joined the dance. Ceasing to be a spectator, I might not have *seen* the dancers; flowers no doubt of Eton, Wycombe Abbey, Roedean, their thoughts determined by *The Times*, a Scottish nurse, their school or 'Daddy the JP'. But in those moments when I lingered beside their shifting kaleidoscope, I thought them celestial. There was nothing celestial about the howl with which Barbara greeted the hunting horns of the final gallop. Mongols find a good brass fanfare irresistible. She escaped our clutches and 'tantivy, tantivy' was gathered up at the stroke of midnight, into the dance. Although her wild cries of 'Cocky-locky, Cocky-locky', 'a Rabbit bit me' were distinctly audible, no adverse comment was made and Lord Rampion returned her to our table with serene courtesy.

Learning to drink, I learnt to speak and move spontaneously, chemically speaking. I knew Mother was against it – she had, I believe, been a member of the Band of Hope – so on my second vacation from Cambridge, I prised up one of the floorboards in my bedroom and made a cache for bottles. There was a dance in aid of the Mission to Seamen in the Parish Hall and my sister and I were to go with the son and daughter of Judge and Lady Pourinson. I lifted my board, sucked back about a quarter of Scotch and joined the company, who were having a discreet sherry, in the drawing-room.

Although in later years, I remember my father questioning me about the number of women I had known, and groaning with horror and fascination as 'One, two, three, four, five, etc,' I ticked them off on my fingers, at the time he had little belief in my sexual prowess – or compulsions. He took me aside for a tip.

'Freda, my boy, now there's a girl! If I was your age, she wouldn't slip through my fingers!'

As Freda turned a good thirteen stone the metaphor was not entirely happy; but I knew only too well what he was concerned with: Freda was the daughter of a judge and a rich, titled woman.

Something inside me began plotting. Once at the Hall I picked up the daughter of a local publican, whisked her round the floor a couple of times and then up to the balcony. I cannot remember the girl's name, I did not touch her, but I did talk! Though a trifle flattered by my attentions, the poor creature must have been bored stiff. On and on went the monologue, Lady Pourinson scowled, Mother hollered up to the balcony, 'Come down, darling, what are you doing up there?' Freda moped, Eliel fumed, but like young Lochinvar, 'I recked not.'

I returned a little after the rest of the party and collapsed into my bedroom chair, happy and fuddled. Mother came in first, in her nightgown, distinctly *décolletée*.

'Tommy, what have you done to me, what have you done to all of us?'

I made no comment since I was savouring somewhat drunkenly the taste of freedom and it was remarkably pleasant. Eliel appeared next and was really furious. He was armed with a walking-stick and brandishing his weapon shouted, 'What I don't know is whether you are fool or a knave.'

'Both of them,' I replied, 'but bugger off, please, please do!'

'How dare you speak to me like that, me your father, the rector of this parish. Do you know what you've done, you've disgraced your mother and me, disgraced us publicly, not to mention your sister and the Pourinsons.'

He advanced with a very unpleasant expression, but I wasn't as drunk as all that and didn't like the look of his stick. I swerved past him, whisked up to my bedroom, got my .22 rifle, loaded it and went out by the back stairs into the garden. It was pleasant to stroll in the night like this, down small flower-scented paths, well-armed too, and with the whisky still warm inside me. I would take my time, dawdle around a bit, and when I returned to the house, Eliel would be safely in bed and snoring.

I had underestimated the man. When I returned to the door, there he was, complete with walking-stick.

'You've been after her again, after that trollop. And now you've come back to batten on us. Well, I'm going to show you.'

This was our 'moment of Truth'. He raised his walking-stick.

I raised my gun and very deliberately – I have never, except when 'tried in the extreme' been one for final solutions, fired, at the stone of the door, some six or seven inches to the left of his right ear. No doubt there is still a little splintered 'nick' in the stonework of the vicarage. That was the end of Eliel's dominance. He bolted up to his bedroom, turned the key in his door and did not reappear till the following morning. He must have been up before me though. When I came down with shame and a mild hangover (the two are closely related) my rifle had disappeared, so had the sword of great-grandfather Blackburn and his two rapiers which used to adorn the hall. Eliel was taking no chances and had cornered the arsenal.

Aunt Marion was with us at the time and her serene presence at the breakfast table comforted me and mollified Adelaide, though it probably strengthened Eliel's conviction that there was no possible solution except my banishment to a colony, the very furthest, and as soon as possible. She listened to his imprecations with bland indifference.

'Well, Marion,' he said after describing my pot-shot, 'what am I going to do about the fellow?'

'What do you mean by "fellow". Thomas is a Fenwick, my dear Eliel, the Fenwicks have always been accustomed to firearms.'

A remarkable sophism; no wonder my poor father was furious!

'And I'm a Blackburn and let me tell you, Marion, the Blackburns were messengers for King James.'

'Really, Eliel, may I tell you that the Fenwicks have never run messages for anyone! They may have received them.'

'The boy will have to work. He can't fritter away his time in knavery, he will have to stop fouling his own nest, go to a university, get a degree. He must go to Durham.'

'Durham?'

'Yes, you heard what I said, the University of Durham. My university. It was good enough for me.'

'Your . . . wife . . . my sister Adelaide and I, had always thought Cambridge was the best place for Thomas.'

Eliel looked furiously at Adelaide. Things really were on the boil and no doubt he had a word with her later since the following morning Marion left.

That at the age of eighteen I qualified for Cambridge had nothing to do with Weaver and everything with Colonel Stonehouse,
a retired officer of the Indian Army. He looked rather like Beatrix Potter's Tommy Brock and bestowed on me a gentleness,
sympathy and educational wisdom for which I shall never cease
to be grateful. 'Responsions' or 'Little Go' are perhaps negligible
in comparison with the standards of modern education which
require the young to absorb and then regurgitate within the space
of three hours, topics which merit a lifetime's study. Still Colonel
Stonehouse did get me into Cambridge. Only by achievement can
one face those psychic difficulties which otherwise would be intolerable; since he enabled me to pass my examinations, the Colonel
was the first person who showed me how to come to terms with
myself. Marion always thought of me as a Fenwick and was, at that
time, the only relative who had some understanding of my particular problems and difficulties. Her opinion was not shared by Featherstone Fenwick, my mother's brother, who by acquisitiveness
and business acumen had increased his share of the family fortune
until he owned a grouse moor, a Rolls Royce and the greater part
of the countryside north of Wolsingham. He gained considerable
satisfaction from riding on a stout cob to the highest point of his
domain and noting that with one exception he was monarch of
all he surveyed. The exception was caused by an obstinate peasant
who refused to sell his small plot of land, plumb in the middle of
Uncle's moor. Not only that, but when the beaters were driving
grouse towards the butts where Uncle, his friends, their dogs and
loaders waited to give the birds a warm reception, he would set
up nets and reap a rich harvest of these saleable wingborne meals.

At Uncle's house the hospitality, though teetotal, was lavish, the
guests rich, the conversation for the most part a regurgitation of
The Times. There was another favourite topic of this clan – family
resemblances.

'Guy, there, now he's the spit and image of old Tom Muschamp
who used to farm over at Heatherley.'

'You're right, Will, and just look at Sonia.' Featherstone pointed
at his grand-daughter. 'There's old Aunt Harriet for you. Once
swung a gander over a wall by its neck!'

I noted that this particular conversation always passed briskly over myself and this confirmed my feeling of unreality at the Lodge; of being invisible. No doubt a remark of Featherstone's explains why I was left out of 'Family Resemblances'.

'Eliel,' he announced over the whisky bottle which was produced surreptitiously when the women had left the room, 'says he's sallow because of biliousness. Bilious my foot, we know better than that!'

I did not understand the significance of that remark or the gust of laughter which followed it. However when I entered Cambridge a few weeks later the sense of being inferior and invisible went into abeyance. I had an identity, I was an undergraduate of an ancient university.

Not that there was anything ancient about my own college. It was a vast Victorian affair of red brick devoted to the mass-production of school teachers and potential clerics. It would have been pleasant to have entered an older place but Father knew the Master who had previously been a Canon of some north country cathedral. Fulsome had written a book called *Christ, Sex and Modern Youth* and would keep an eye on me. His first words were:

'Blackburn, I know your father and am very happy to have you in our little community.' His last, 'I am sending you down, sir, as from nine a.m. tomorrow morning – for the sake of my college.' Since it was dislike at first sight we had no intervening conversation.

Eliel also arranged my course of studies. I was extremely anxious to read English, but this subject, he told me, was vague, imaginative and quite beyond my parochial intelligence. Law was the thing; it was merely a question of mugging up hard facts – any fool could do it. Moreover, once qualified, my future was assured; Uncle Cathgart had promised to take me as a junior partner into his firm of solicitors. Eliel had certainly got something taped: but it wasn't life. That I managed to pass the First and Second Year examinations in a subject in which I had no scrap of interest was an achievement. But indifference to the Law deepened my alienation from the University, and all that now remains of my studies is the case of Rex *v.* Beard. The gentleman in question had intercourse with a goose and since congress with birds did not at the time come under the heading of Bestiality, added a new article to the legal canon.

Having worked for many years in various places of education and noted the extreme, at times excessive care that is now given to the personal problems of the young, I realize that we live in the post-Freudian Age and it is no longer possible to ignore the compulsions of the psyche, its conflicts and vagaries.

At Cambridge in the thirties, they were ignored completely. Dr. Derwent, my personal tutor, a pink-eyed, rabbity man, was an authority on Norse mythology. Students were a frightening intrusion on his life work. There was the Chaplain, but Dr. Goodbody, musty, rusty and evangelical, did not press his invitations to the S.C.M. beyond my third refusal. The Secretary of the Society had a more serious concern for my spiritual welfare. John Makin, a willowy youth, his face blank and pallid, was devoted to God and the 1st College Boat of which he was coxswain. He would often press a friendly tract into my hand and join me for a chat when I ambled back with a bottle of gin from the buttery. He had a trick of staring sideways and nodding at invisible creatures. His conversation was both original and apocalyptic. Some years later I learnt from the *News of the World* that poor Makin, while qualifying for the priesthood, had first strangled, then carved up a pantry boy. The dismembered body had been kept in a trunk under his bed for a number of weeks. The word MINE was inscribed on the chest with a heated poker. In court, he expressed no opinion or emotion other than a strong protest against the prison library. It contained no works of serious theological interest. Even the sanguinary English Law of the time found this attitude a trifle eccentric and I trust Makin is still pursuing his theological studies at Broadmoor.

On my first evening at College I was visited by a number of noisy young men in blazers. They announced that I must join an assortment of clubs, ranging from chess to rowing and Rugby football. I took the line of least resistance and joined the lot but only achieved distinction – it was highly dubious – as an oarsman. When chosen for a place in the second boat of college, I celebrated the honour by a visit to a London nightclub, slept till past midday in the bed of an accommodating hostess and missed the boat.

# Chapter Eleven

*Memento mori*

My ability to visit London nightclubs, entertain as lavishly as I wished, drink excessively, buy expensive suits, ride horses, depended upon the generosity of Aunt Marion. She gave me enough money to foster my neuroses and eccentricities with a Byronic amplitude. Mistaken, but a question of love for all that. Aunt Marion disliked Eliel and was deeply concerned that as a child I was so vulnerable to his whims and obsessions.

At the end of her life, with the trust we shared and the confessional urgency of the dying, she told me about my unfortunate father. I was on leave at the time, and our twilight communion was one of those times when the curtain lifts and almost, it seems, one knows reality.

'You see, my dear,' she said, obese, dignified, tranquil. 'I couldn't do much for you, there was Adelaide to think of, but I did what I could.'

'You did a great deal.'

We were alone in the house of Aunt June where Marion lived when, to her grief and irritation, she was too old and ill to stay in her own home. My family were up there at the time. She had lent it to us for the holiday and every morning would come up with a large chicken, a brace of guinea fowl or an enormous and indigestible cake. But this was my last day and under the oil paintings of her ancestors, plain but resolute, the Italian Madonna, the beautifully bound books of Grandfather Thomas, she talked on. She told me how again and again she would arrive at the vicarage determined on a lengthy stay and each time found it intolerable and had to leave after two or three days.

'My dear Thomas, I could not bear it. He would taunt you. You would answer back, then he would drag you off to the study and thrash you. The sound of that strap. I did protest but if I had said what I really felt then he would never have allowed me in the house again. I had to give you the presents I brought – on the sly; it was intolerable. Adelaide, poor creature, she was under his . . . thumb. I knew I must go on seeing you children, I was determined you should stay with me in the summer holidays. So I kept silence . . . and left . . .'

'I do understand.'

'Of course you do, my dear,' she stretched out her hand and took mine: a gesture somewhat unusual in her stoical family. The talk continued and to my surprise I learnt that she had supported the match between my mother and father and been fond of Eliel at first.

'It was the way he treated you . . .'

She lay back in her chair, exhausted for a few moments, her eyes closed.

'We did look forward to your visits. I think our holidays with you were the best times for all of us.'

'Were they, darling, I'm so glad and now,' she glanced at the great clock, 'it is time for you to go.'

'I can stay another hour, the taxi isn't coming till seven-thirty.'

'You must be with your family. Go along with you, my dear, and goodbye. I shan't see you again.'

'Of course you will, I shall be coming to Wolsingham after my next trip.' Aunt Marion got very slowly and heavily from her chair and arm-in-arm we walked to the door. She turned there and kissed me.

'I know what I'm saying, Thomas, and it's quite all right. I shan't see you here again. Now goodbye, my dear, and God bless you.'

I left her and, God forgive me, with a certain hope that her prophecy might run true. Marion was a rich woman and I was one of her heirs. But though feelings are mixed and one of mine was squalid self-interest, this does not lessen my respect and devotion for this remarkable woman. It is after their dying that our feelings towards those we knew when alive achieve, not a final clarity, but a moment of relative truth which either permits the relationship to grow or ends it. My dialogue with Aunt Marion is by no means finished.

She was dead when six months later I returned. But with that gross if well-meaning materialism which can refuse to believe that death is the goal of life and an old woman of more than ninety years might well wish to die, they had kept her alive as long as possible. Far be it from me to attribute unworthy motives to Dr. Lemon's holding Marion back from her wished-for goal. It is the duty of a physician to preserve life and his daily visits of ten to fifteen minutes were not particularly expensive. Still one could wish he had paid some attention to the patient, who paid him. Aunt Marion's last words after her final saline injection were, 'I want to go, why don't they let me?'

Perhaps it was the example of her sister that made Adelaide so resolute for death when stricken by cancer of the lung at the age of eighty-five. Mind you, Eliel, who though bed-ridden long before his wife, went 'slowly' and survived her by some years, would never believe this complaint was the immediate cause of Adelaide's departure. It was associated in his mind with the Evil Eye and divine nemesis and I suspect he may have bullied the little doctor who gave the verdict into changing the death certificate into 'bronchitis'. He was formidable even in his bath chair.

Eliel gave death a good run for his money and found it hard to believe in Adelaide's. Even when he did realize that she was dying, one of his main concerns was that she should either wear her faded wig or a small mob cap. The Fenwicks were rather short of hair and he did not wish the thin silvery locks of his dying wife to be seen. There was something of *The American Way of Death* in this desire to keep up appearances.

Mother was very active until her final year. She persisted in believing that Eliel, who suffered from Parkinson's disease and found extreme difficulty in walking, was, in point of fact, a malingerer – for whom she had a certain tenderness. He certainly did play it up a bit, but her humming of a brisk Scottish air as she pushed forward a man who really was enduring nervous confusion, not to mention her conviction that the various medical remedies for his malady were in fact its cause, were by no means helpful. 'If only he wouldn't take those things they give him,' she pronounced, convinced that the medical profession were responsible for her husband's palsy and determined to create a nation of drug-addicts.

As she grew older, Adelaide gave to her children an increasing affection and understanding. She read the reviews of my books, she listened to the occasional reading of my verse on the radio, she loved and criticized her grandchildren, she accosted perambulators and enthused over their occupants, she cried with joy (and misunderstanding) when a play of mine was produced on the radio. She also continued to garden expertly until her last months. Her gardening was linked with an extreme fondness for birds, which she once suggested (her religious views were a trifle unorthodox) might well be the departed souls of human beings. Certainly they would come flying down to her whistle and scraps. Adelaide also read Boswell and various biographies and helped to attend to my father. His needs were unceasing and he had installed an appalling bell which could rouse you from sleep like a kick in the stomach.

In order to go into the future, Adelaide had to absorb her past life into her present moment of being; so she ruminated on the past. I shared these explorations of her finished time and in consequence, at one remove, her intention to die. Death started on an autumn morning. She understood the pain in her left lung more accurately than her doctors and announced that she had no intention of being 'treated' at home. Despite a racking cough, she dressed herself with extreme neatness, packed her suitcase and walked without assistance to the ambulance which took her to the local hospital. There she refused a private ward. She also refused to deny the intention towards death which had now become for her an expression of creative life. Both Matron and the sisters considered Adelaide a bad patient.

'We try to help her, Mr. Blackburn, but what can we do? I ask you, what can we do?'

That question, since she refused injections and with a keen blue stare poured their other remedies into the chamber pot, was difficult to answer. But I did smuggle a number of half bottles of brandy into the ward. Though a temperate woman, in her last days Mother gained considerable solace from alcohol and the reputation among a number of Draconian sisters, creaking in starched linen, of being an addict. They were under a misapprehension. They would have done better to have given her the hot-water bottle she asked for. I regret that I did not battle more strenuously for this 'dangerous' article. She was cold and dying – it was her last personal wish.

As if stripped by death of her irrelevancies, whether of class or race, Mother did make one sincere friendship in hospital. It was with an African nurse of extreme blackness and rotundity.

'Nurse Nukba, now she does understand.'

What Nukba and Mother understood thoroughly annoyed the Matron who believed it was a question of unlawful gossip.

'A dear little girl died this morning,' Adelaide said. 'I visited her, she was only six, but she has gone over, and do you know, they carried her, covered with flowers, right through this ward, past me. I think her name was . . . no . . . no, I can't remember but she has gone over.'

When I repeated this statement to the Matron, she did not actually say that Adelaide was a witch, but her looks implied it. Either that or the black nurse had been chattering. Since Nurse Nukba had been off duty for a couple of days and no little corpse was ever carried through the geriatric ward, I feel that, working her way out of time and space, and without sensory evidence, Adelaide was aware of the child's dying. For a child did die and at the time she mentioned.

How can you know about death until you have experienced it? My mother's death was long and arduous – a difficult birth. At times she would speak to me, or to her other children, at times to her father, to Marion and Aunt Jenny, speaking with a cheerful intimacy.

'She's wandering now, it won't be long,' said the Sister, as Mother murmured, 'Well, Jenny, how nice to see you.' Or staring through my sisters and me, 'Father, Father . . . and you, Marion dear, but we shouldn't have let. . . . O Jenny I am sorry . . .'

She slid further and further out of time, came back to me, one moment in the peristalsis of her birth into death, and then withdrew as a person from the movement of her lungs and heart. She was a strong woman and these organs went on for many hours after she had left them. Her process of dying was long and thorough.

'Dear Thomas,' she would say, 'dear Sylvia, dear John,' as we sat beside her bed and she grasped our hands firmly. Then, 'Yes, Father, I do hear you. Wait a minute though. Yes, Father . . .' She was puzzled; entering the world of death, we of the living world were the ghosts that haunted her. She passed for increasing minutes out of her body; no doubt the long-drawn snoring of Adelaide's lungs, the rattle, the inarticulate 'aaak, aah, aah', the jerking head, are what are known as 'the terrors of death'. They were the pangs by which she was born into death. In those last hours she teetered backward and forward between time and eternity until finally she slid out of time and a great shudder marked the completeness of her withdrawal.

Her last words were about the woman who has become my wife and about whom, since I did not wish to burden her with the break-up of a marriage, I had said nothing.

'Tell Margaret,' she said, 'that I am very grateful to her for making you a good home. Give her my love.'

She bequeathed the retinae of her eyes to any hospital that might find them of value, and her body, if it was of interest, to medical research. She asked that no stone should be her irrelevant memorial.

# Chapter Twelve

Light thickens . . .

SHAKESPEARE, *Macbeth*

Aunt Marion's devotion was a mixed blessing. She was a rich woman and equally generous with her cash and affections. The cheque for £200 she sent me at the beginning of each term was a secret between us. Added to my mother's substantial allowance I was able to gratify most of my fancies. Unfortunately, I was unfamiliar with mountaineering and did not spend my substance on visits to Chamonix or Zermatt but on London nightclubs, parties, alcohol, whores.

A waste, but there is no point in lamenting the past. Given one's nature and nurture most follies seem inevitable. The prodigal son must make the dark journey if he is to return to himself and whatever is signified by the word 'father'. I used to think this parable was a useful tract for reforming convicts, but Christ's sayings seem to me now – among many other things – a unique exploration of those invisible, uncodified laws which determine our psyche and behaviour. Perhaps the 'fatted calf' slain for the prodigal means that experience, however apparently disastrous, can be of value if at long last it gains the lucidity of understanding.

Still desires do not always fit in with the ability to gratify them. Some years later, though devoted to rock-climbing, I was on a very slender budget, bought secondhand boots, nailed them myself, used the cheapest rope and slept in a small tent which was by no means waterproof and without a sleeping bag. I also had to hitch-hike up to Wales, Scotland or the Lake District, a task I loathed and was bad at. After the third or fourth rejection, my face gained an expression of restrained but paranoid fury which did not encourage motorists. The Alps were financially impossible until much later when I had lost that complete confidence on rock and

ice which is synonymous with a belief in the absolute value of
the sport. At Cambridge, I could have financed a small Himalayan
expedition. However, if introduced to rock-climbing in those days
I might well have been indifferent. What mattered was an intense
no-man's land, imaginative, submarine, between the everyday
world and madness.

They remind me, these four or so years, at Cambridge and
after, of that period of childhood when my life was dominated
by dreams, and it was hard to distinguish between the experience of sleep and waking. But there was a difference: now I was
living the dream, or rather the dream was living me. The details
of behaviour, as I moved like a sleep-walker through the byways
of an academic world, were often petty and sordid. But what
mattered was vision and it was more often infernal than celestial.
Events, whether it was a question of some town girl I encountered on a bridge, the perception of gaslight burning on the mist
of a famous river, entering the cave of a nightclub, each hostess
magical as Koré by her dim-lit table, were the mere precipitates of
uncircumscribed revelation. What I remember of my first sexual
encounter is not so much the girl herself as the strangeness of two
people meeting and after a few minutes embarking on this voyage
in a shared body. I could hardly see Mabel's face in the dusk and
her voice is mingled with the sound of lapping water. Not that
our rendezvous was particularly romantic. There were fishbones
under the boat house and other less savoury objects. Nor was our
bodily intercourse of particular significance. But I was delighted
when we resorted to a pub and seeing my face clearly for the first
time, she chirruped, 'Coo, aren't you lovely, got a profile just like
Ivor Novello. You can be my steady and have it for nothing.'

I had no desire to be anybody's 'steady', but Mabel's remark
was a real enhancement of my *amour impropre*. Narcissus had
found himself and he had a 'lovely profile'. It was, of course, the
bleaching, the chin drill, the verdict of 'mere animal' which made
the praise of a young woman who supplemented her earnings in
Woolworths by a little prostitution, of such importance.

Later, I met Jeanette, a handsome Swiss girl of some feeling and
character. I had no intention of 'being involved' with anyone and

it was just her understanding and capacity for relationship which made me incapable of consummating this affair. Like Dowson, I was faithful in a fashion – to my own fantasies! Girls of the town made few inroads and with them I had no 'trouble'. Whether or not a cash payment was involved, little tenderness was asked for, only some brisk conversation, a few drinks, a well oiled and vigorous journey through the Tunnel of Love, the price of a taxi.

There were exceptions. A young woman who worked in a café was much admired by the undergraduates. Then as now, Beardsley's drawings corresponded to the erotic fantasies of some students. Marigold had sharp pointed teeth, very red gums, slanted eyes and a blend of innocence and depravity which would have delighted the youthful master. Perhaps she was too close to some denizen of my unconscious to be a 'playmate'. Certainly when I had her alone to myself, it was not merely a surfeit of drink made me incapable of an erection, rush to the lavatory and vomit. Some months later in London, I had a similar experience with a dark and lacquered Creole not unlike Medusa. It may well be impossible to have intercourse with women who are associated with certain images of the unconscious.

When I returned from the lavatory – pale and sweating – Marigold, clothed and smoking a cigarette, looked very cross indeed. It had not been her idea of a pleasant evening!

'Well, you'd better get me a taxi, now hadn't you?'

Feeling far from well, I complied. However, when I saw her getting into the cab, Eros reasserted himself. I yelled to the driver to wait and since it was impossible to get out of college after nine p.m., started to scale the side gate by the library. Getting to the top, since I am a natural climber, was simple enough. But there the trouble started. The prudent clerics who planned the place had taken a tip from Dartmoor – or vice versa. The upper bar of the gate not only revolved but was armed with close-set circles of spikes. The whole contraption was kept well-oiled by the College porter – Canon Fulsome was a stickler for details – and spun round at the lightest touch. I had been over the thing two or three times before and knew the technique; but on this occasion I was very drunk indeed. I gained the proper foothold in the small gap between the iron bar and the library wall. Next one had to grasp one of the iron spikes and, pressing down on it, hold it upright while one swung the other leg over to the lower ironwork. After that the descent was simple. But my hand could not keep that spike steady. At the crucial moment it spun round and flung me backward, my jacket caught on a lower point of the door, held for a second, then tore apart and I plunged face forward some fifteen feet to the gravel. I was lucky not to have castrated myself by this peccadillo; as it is I still have a slightly distorted lip and a memory of the blood and grit which I tasted next morning on a soaked pillow.

My room servant was devoted, if not to myself, to the substantial tips I gave him at frequent intervals. He called up my doctor who gave me an anti-tetanus injection and removed the grit from my lacerated and swollen lip, he fed me in my rooms for a few days and took care that no word came to the College authorities. When I did return into circulation, neither Dr. Derwent, Canon Fulsome, nor the chaplain remarked or inquired of my appearance. They did, if I remember, wince slightly as they passed me in their gowns on the way to evening service.

At the end of my fourth term, Nigel Hantworth, who had been both my crony and disciple – he was a very disturbed youth – experienced a nervous breakdown and left College. Nervous breakdowns are now a recognized call for aid in some psychological dilemma. At that time, since largely unrecognized, they had to be dramatic. Nigel came to morning service very drunk indeed, he muttered curses during the first prayer, he groaned and stamped during the Benedictus, he started to scream during the lesson and while my other friend, John Home, vamped on the organ – he was always good in an emergency – was carried out of chapel, roaring. I believe he told the Master that I had encouraged him to drink and had been largely responsible for his downfall. No doubt, like most addicts, I wished to lessen the solitude and inferiority of my addiction by gaining converts. That the Master said nothing to me about Nigel's statements is remarkable since he was a conscientious man. No doubt, he did not wish to talk about anything he found disturbing, still, as I learnt later, he kept all these things and pondered them in his heart.

He had something to ponder about a few weeks later! I celebrated my twenty-first birthday by a small, select party. There was
Larkin, the son of a breakfast cereal king who imagined, quite
mistakenly, that I was his entry to polite society, there was John
Home and three semi-professional women of the town. At two
a.m., a time when it was quite impossible to enter or leave the
College – the girls were in no position to do a bit of gate climbing
– we escorted them through intricate and spurious cloisters to
Fulsom's house. We presented them with a £5 note, told them
that the Master ran a late-night taxi service and would for a very
reasonable sum run them home. Again, no comment was made.
No doubt Fulsome had his suspicions but he was probably so
horrified by the appearance of three whores at the Master's Lodge
in the small hours that he slammed the door, bolted it and didn't
emerge till morning.

I am not astonished by my callous lack of feeling with women.
The early involvement with Adelaide had been so stifling that it
might well have caused inversion or impotence. Feeling was associated with Mother and in consequence an extreme danger. For
many years my relationship with women was a resolute adoration
of a romantic ideal – largely based upon myself. I also had sexual
intercourse whenever possible but refused to be tied down by one
strand of feeling. This divorce of feeling from the sexual relationship may have strengthened my concern for poetry. Eliot writes:

'Lips that would kiss form prayers to broken stone.'

Perhaps only in the later forties and with my second wife did I
achieve a relationship based on some understanding and tolerance
rather than fantasy and compulsion.

Not that my first marriage was for a number of years unsatisfactory. On leave during the last war, I found it impossible to get a
climbing companion since all my friends who rock-climbed were
involved with Hitler. Someone mentioned Eugenie D'Arembert.
She was attractive and athletic. She worked at the Admiralty and
since her uncle was an Admiral, might well get off for some days
at a moment's notice. The happiness I experienced was determined, in part, by Eugenie's aptitude for climbing. On our second

day in the Lakes she seconded me – a little traction was needed – up Pisgah Buttress Direct – a severe climb. On the third of those sunlit, perpetual, bird-haunted days we climbed the New West and Rib and Slab on Pillar Rock and – for the first time – went to bed together. The fact that we also shared the more dangerous sport exorcized for a time my fear of feeling and for some years I could love Eugenie with sincerity.

There was no fear in climbing, only anxiety lest rain might make the harder routes impossible. There was delight in the gulf of air below me and the sense that moving above that gulf by small wrinkles and cracks of the granite I was not only holding my life safely in my hands, but gathering myself into myself. At the end of a climb, I experienced greater strength and confidence than I had ever known. Personal relationships were tenuous and complicated, so were examinations and the business of earning a living, but the fact that I had ascended Jones Route on Scafell from Lords Rake with security and certainty was a real achievement. Eugenie followed up these routes on our honeymoon with admirable courage and skill. The climax of our holiday was Botterills Slab, a climb still regarded as very severe in these more technical days of slings and Karabiners.

I also liked Eugenie's painting. Indeed at the start of our relationship, her art, love of music, and artistic friends were a delight. Later they became a pain in the neck. But though Eugenie's concern for painting was one cause of the breakdown of our marriage, a more compelling cause was my increasing devotion to poetry. Although an impersonal and spiritual process, the poetic 'muse' can easily if falsely be associated with some particular person. Invested with the glamour of the Muse, any woman can become the White Goddess. But the glamour soon fades and the love-life of a number of poets have been serials. After three good, sober years of marriage and teaching, I did dream (despite critics of Mr. Graves's theory) and dream night after night of an ecstatic woman with whom I must be united both in time and eternity to achieve wholeness and inspiration. She (it was a kind of 'he' in one case!) soon began to play hell with my marriage though a good deal of verse came out of her manifestations. There was Madame Therber, rich, a devotee of the arts. In poem after poem I celebrated my rapport with this clairvoyant and promiscuous woman. Later I encountered a small French poetess and imagined for a few weeks that with her I had achieved a union of soul and body. There was also a male novelist of very considerable reputation. When I first met him, he was living with a somewhat nebulous political figure who had left his wife and family for the sake of his homosexual friend. For a few weeks, Eugenie, the novelist, myself and his friend would meet in their impressive studio house. But when his 'Arthur' died, John Edginton became increasingly more absorbed in the strange and twisted compulsions of his life from which came those novels which catch, with the brevity of great art, certain moments of progressive terror, and strip the mask from the human being, to show the 'creature' itself – spirit and animal. I became increasingly fonder of John. He gave me confidence in my own work which had received no recognition, and he increased my awareness of that 'tragic significance' of life. Yet, though a religious writer, he purported to loathe religion and would dismiss Christ with, 'Oh don't talk to me about that old queen; we all know what she was up to.'

I had no desire for Rupert Brooke's 'rough, male kiss of blankets', and found the idea of physical contact without interest. Nor did I find his remedy for depression – it was sodomy – particularly relevant. Our relationship fell apart. But I shall always remember our friendship and the enhancement of my capacity to see and to feel which came from it.

Obviously, Eugenie found these inroads on our married life difficult. That it lasted for some sixteen years does suggest a certain mutual understanding. It also depended upon our daughter of whom we are both extremely fond.

The relationship cancelled itself out but it did have feeling. In this sense it had few predecessors. There was Eve Back, a hostess in a nightclub. Not that I did not wish for a little variety but, 'I know what you want, Eve, eh, you rascal!' Madame would gurgle from the depths of her enormous besequinned bosom. She was a motherly soul, and dismissing my suggestion that Eve could probably do with one night's rest 'off duty', got the girl over, presto, by telephone. So Eve it was and I achieved quite an understanding with this gentle and undemanding whore. I remember our quiet bed-ridden conversation, her surprise that I did not demand a more exacting response for the cheque I made out each morning (£2, and it included an excellent breakfast and accommodation in her bed for the night). I also remember that whore or not she was a very amiable woman.

My companion on these visits to London was John Home, a talented if somewhat overpowering youth, the College organ scholar, and now a successful composer. He shared my contempt for the students of our college, and we got ourselves thoroughly disliked. Our camel-hair coats, suede shoes and green hats, the rave garb of the time, might not have been conspicuous at other colleges, but they were quite out of place among the sports jackets, flannel bags and college mufflers of the embryonic clerics. One afternoon we entertained a Negro pianist and singer in John's rooms. There were cocktails and a certain amount of music. Word got round though, and when we escorted our colourful guests to their car, we were hissed and booed by an assembly of the righteous who, in the best tradition, flung a number of small stones.

I had worked hard for just such a reaction. Whether it was that of Byron, Rimbaud, Lord George Hell, I had to assume some role to mask my inferiority. If I had been studying English, inferiority might have been tempered by some achievement. I did read widely and Huysmans, Oscar Wilde and De Sade were balanced by Dostoevsky, Virginia Woolf and Chekhov. The authority of the English Department might have supported such reading and lessened my alienation from the university.

The jurists seemed impossible. I found it increasingly difficult to absorb their enormous diet of fact, arid and irrelevant, then regurgitate the stuff upon foolscap. To avoid boredom I tried a few variations. But Dr. Ling, an authority on international law, was not pleased when I changed the theme of our bi-weekly essay from 'Machiavelli and the Authority of Nations', to 'The Legal Implications of Dostoevsky's *Crime and Punishment*'.

'You did put down our title, Mr. Blackburn?'

'Yes, Dr. Ling.'

'Then why did you inflict this very personal flight of fancy upon me? I am a hard-working if humdrum member of the legal department of this University and have no time to peruse fiction.'

I ceased to attend lectures but did mug up the appropriate books and managed to pass my second year examination. It was at a price. The weeks in which I had sweltered over the manipulation of Real Property and the Laws of Tort created an invincible repugnance for the subject. In my third year, like a horse that refuses to go over a fence, my unconscious shied away. Try as I might, it was impossible to read another word of Law. But Law was my reason for being at Cambridge, and deprived of this reason I started a steep glide downwards. Before this blockage I tried to believe that although a trifle erratic, life did have a goal. At long last I would 'eat my dinners', 'enter chambers', becoming a practising barrister. Now, since there was a sense of utter inertia if I so much as opened a book of jurisprudence, such achievements were out of the question.

Reading went on: Roger Fry, Aldous Huxley, Clive Bell, Lytton Strachey, T. S. Eliot. But my sense that these authors were a mere delinquent sideline from serious life was confirmed by Eliel.

One vacation he got hold of my copy of *The Waste Land* and capering up and down the rectory corridors chanted:

> 'Rats' feet over broken glass . . .
> Rats' feet, rats' feet, rats' feet . . .'

'And listen to this Adelaide' (she had appeared with a jug of barley water):

> 'To Carthage then I came
> Burning
> O Lord thou pluckest me out
> Burning.'

He chortled with glee. Youth has no innate certainty as to its own judgment. What reason had I to believe that his scorn of this great religious poet was both fatuous and moronic? Capering in that corridor, my book in his hand, he would have been supported in his scorn by most of the jurists. That was the vacation before my last term at Cambridge. When I returned to the place in October, something other than myself had decided to put an end to the fiasco.

Unable to believe in the social relevance of imagination, to give love or friendship, I had worked out a betwixt-between role that was unloving, savage but in a crude way, imaginative. In the role of Lord George Hell I once came to dinner in full evening dress, armed with a riding crop and attempted to whip a student who had been one of the stone throwers. Herriot did not believe in 'blabbing' and the incident was hushed up.

The immediate cause of my dismissal from Cambridge was a contraceptive, used apparently, and found under the window of my ground-floor bedroom. The finder called a meeting of his fellow Christians. God had at last delivered the wicked into their hands. A happy little band marched off to the Master's House, carrying the article on a scarlet cushion perhaps, or in a tin, perforated to let it breathe.

Fulsome was equally delighted. When I came to the study he had the thing on a large white plate.

'Do you see this, Blackburn?'

I bent down to look. 'Yes, sir.'

'No doubt you know what it is?'

'A form of contraception, we call it a French Letter. The French, I believe, refer to it as *une capote anglaise*.'

The Master flushed with anger.

'Believe me, sir, I'm not here to bandy words with you! For three, no two years and some months I have endured your, your . . . malpractices, not for your sake but for the sake of your devout father. Now the time has come, you must go.'

The word 'father' did it. Fulsome was collecting not only gramophone records but china dogs. The room was full of them. With extraordinary adroitness, he dodged the first and second little brute but I got him with the third as he was whisking through the door.

Safely on the other side and with the key turned, he pronounced, a trifle shakily, 'Tomorrow, sir, and before noon, you leave for the good of my College and you will never return. Never!'

# Chapter Thirteen

*Ah, Seigneur! donnez-moi la force et le courage*
*De contempler mon cœur et mon corps sans dégoût!*
CHARLES BAUDELAIRE

I have no clear recollection of the two years which followed my dismissal from Cambridge and the analysis by a Harley Street psychiatrist which after a few intolerable months when I fought against self-knowledge did bring me back to some reality and integration.

The time-stream was broken. There is no continuity of happening, only isolated events, fractured, and terrible, looming out of amnesia. When my parents were summoned to Cambridge I was in a nursing home but have no memory of how I got there. At that time I did not feel or think or drink. I lay hunched up on a floor or bed in the appropriate foetal position. I rocked backwards and forwards and repeated over and over again two words 'aakh – mehan, aakh – mehan'. They were adapted, I believe, from a film called *The Mummy* in which Boris Karloff after a few happy weeks out of the tomb, lamented his enforced return to a sarcophagus. Canon Fulsome did tell my parents that I was deeply disturbed and in need of a long period of psychological treatment. But despite the nursing home and my dismissal from Cambridge Adelaide and Eliel were determined to believe there was nothing seriously wrong. It was just a question of bad company and alcohol. In future both would be avoided. Their ostrich-like behaviour was confirmed by my Cambridge doctor, a burly rugger Blue.

'That lad's all right, Canon and Mrs. Blackburn. Keep an eye on him. You have good air in Durham. That's what he needs, fresh air, nourishing food, exercise.'

Certainly when we were on the Flying Scotsman, Eliel did keep an eye on me. Any excursion from our carriage might lead to the bar, and he tailed me. After a visit to the lavatory, there he was outside the door. There was real concern in this but no scrap of understanding. To admit my disturbance would have meant admitting their own sour predicament and that neither Adelaide nor Eliel was prepared to do. Their restricted vision was confirmed by Dr. Buchanan. He had never heard of Freud but would attend the rectory every day to administer a shot of strychnine and collect his ten shillings.

It was to my bedroom in the rectory that I returned. It overlooked the Church and a graveyard made remarkable by one large and three small stones. They bore no inscription but commemorated an unfortunate woman who had murdered her three illegitimate children, then taken her own life. They were smuggled into consecrated ground by an enlightened cleric who believed that suffering was the way of purgation and could manifest itself through disastrous happenings. Even murder and suicide might lead to God.

Besides Buchanan, Uncle also came to the rescue. I remember his stocky figure in green plus-fours beside my bed. He looked at me very critically from a bloodshot eye then turned to Eliel under the impression that I was past hearing.

'You can see the trouble here, Eliel my boy, it's the drink, the demon drink, and you and I have got to get him off it.'

Eliel nodded agreement. He knew all about demons and told me some weeks later that he had actually encountered some in my college rooms. They had pushed against him as he tried to retrieve my belongings. 'Then I knew what the Devil was, a great gust of evil forcing me backwards.'

I wish the gust had been strong enough to keep him away from my bronze snake, Picasso print and Beardsley engravings. They were very bad ju-ju! He stamped the snake flat, burnt the print and engravings and deposited the lot into the fireplace; a prophet casting down the idols of Baal.

The first step in my rehabilitation was financed by Uncle. John Walters was not only a Wesleyan minister but a fisherman. He would 'put me right'. I remember the man who rowed our boat upon Loch Leven, a singularly inept flogging of the water with large colourful flies, and an equally colourful string of platitudes which reached their climax on our last evening. There was a sunset.

Walters pointed at it.

'Do you see that, Blackburn, do you see that?'

'Yes,' I replied, fearing the worst.

'The wonder and glory of it, the wonder and the glory.' For one dreadful moment I thought the Minister was going to get down on his knees in full view of the hotel. However, rhetoric won the day. 'Can a man behold those colours without believing in the might and power of the Supreme Artist. Can you, my dear boy?'

'Yes,' I replied.

He gave me a very dirty look. Featherstone had certainly given him a stony bit of ground to work on. However, he had a duty to his old friend and patron.

'You are like your Uncle Featherstone. He also would say nothing. But he would look at those colours, I have seen him look at those colours and his eyes fill with tears. He believes, my dear boy, like you he believes.'

'In the Sun God?' I queried.

Walters did not get the rather blunt point. He was well away now. 'In the very God of very Gods, the God who bodies himself out through all that majesty.'

I had no particular objections to his ideas. It was the way he put them, and I remember spitting into the darkening waters of Loch Leven.

When I returned from this embarrassing trip, I told my parents that a little more exercise would work wonders and they agreed to my making a walking tour. It was to be along the Roman Wall and then to my birth-place in Cumberland. The outward journey went well enough, and I remember standing under Father's portrait in Hensingham Church in a miasma of guilt and unworthiness. Then the unconscious took over.

I went down to the Whitehaven docks. I am uncertain what happened there or where I slept that night. Certainly a day later I booked a room in a little hotel at Keswick. But when I returned after drinking, why did they shoulder me out into the street and throw my rucksack after me? I am on my knees in the dark, vomiting. Groping. It is a question of continuing to exist. There is a man here. His hand on my shoulder, his hand is my help.

'Lodgings?'

'A place for the night.'

'I will lead you.'

A long way. There is no house here. Only grass and a smell of night plants. There is a bank and he pushes me down on it. It is necessary to continue. Make me real, God. I am dissolving in the acid of this wet grass under the rain which burns me. Is it God erect there in the darkness? Why is he kneeling beside me?

Take shape in this mist.

Who are you? What are you fumbling for?

Thy rod and thy staff they comfort me.

Thy rod.

'Turn over, turn over, turn over, turn over.'

'No.'

Now it is morning and I do not know who or where I am. Like the grass I am dripping wet and the knuckles of my right hand are bruised and bloody.

Then the horses. Two of them, great beasts of the shire, bending down and snuffing with curiosity. This is nightmare! They canter down hill and away kicking a spray of water drops behind them. One must continue.

I walk. There is a lake and for the sake of this brilliant water, it is necessary to continue.

I had only enough money to pay the bus fare for some twenty miles and it was after a thirty-mile walk that I came to the Rectory in the twilight. Like a ghost I stood on the lawn outside the french windows. A family conference was in progress and Eliel was striding up and down the drawing-room.

'Even you, Adelaide, even you must agree this cannot continue!' For once I was in hearty agreement. But there is no staying still. One must go up or down, forwards or backwards. In the next six months my direction was back and down; sharply! For two or three months in that time of dereliction I could maintain the passivity of a self-mistrust that had no limit. Then the endless succession of regular meals, the tea parties in which I sat hunched, guilty and silent, became intolerable and the daemon asserted itself. I told mother that unless I had some jaunt – it was like sex and masturbation and she understood that – then I would go off my head. She would give me ten shillings, loan me one of the family cars – we had two at the time – and I would set off for Newcastle. It was '*un voyage au bout de la nuit*'. I had neither confidence in my own energies nor an ego capable of dealing with them. I rabbitted into the nearest pub, dissolved my mind in alcohol, the cheapest and strongest (an appalling 'port-style' brew with the cheerful name of 'Red Biddy'). Then the unconscious got to work. It was indifferent to conversation, sex, vision. It was very much concerned with dying.

Take shape in this mist.

I enter a pub a month after some forgotten night. A woman is seated in a corner on a small stool, she looks up at me, gets to her feet, raises her arm and flings her glass at me. Apparition, when did I meet you? That you will never know: this happened.

What the Unconscious expressed after I had dissolved my ego on those ten-shilling trips to chaos was an intense dislike of the narrow restrictive consciousness of Thomas Blackburn, so incapable of expressing its far-reaching intentions. It preferred immediate death to slow suffocation. But it cannot have been wholly determined to die, since without any help from the conscious mind, it would drive me home to Wolsingham from Newcastle, and with accuracy I presume, since the car was never scraped the morning after.

My parents must have endured intense anxiety in those bad days. Certainly Eliel was disturbed by a report from the district nurse. She had noticed his car parked carefully on the verge of a lane and discovered me asleep on a haystack, reeking of alcohol. However, since my confusion was their confusion, and that they were unwilling to confront, my parents created euphemisms for such conduct. 'Bad company', 'drink', or 'he is a war baby', such terms warded off our shared predicament.

Eliel did decide to leave Wolsingham.

I do not think he had ever liked this place of stolid dalesmen and omniscient Fenwicks. He was anxious to return to the diocese of Newcastle where he was well liked and had done good work. But Heddon-on-the-Wall was a step downward financially and though shielded from the least pinch of poverty by his affluent wife, Eliel believed in money and felt that I had not been helpful.

I had sobered up a trifle when we came to Heddon and, given some psychiatric treatment and the chance of taking a degree in English at another university, even at this stage might have patched up some *modus vivendi*. But I had no self-confidence, and Father dismissed both psychiatry and literature.

'No, no, my boy, we've had trouble enough already, that stuff will get you nowhere.'

I agreed with him.

In later years imagination and some intelligence have secured me a reasonable living and reputation, but Eliel associated my free use of these energies with the devil and disintegration. It was a question of finding just that study in which I could make no possible progress and setting me at it. Since ignorance and malpractice make an indivisible marriage, he did believe that by plunging me back into the law, he was doing the very best that was possible for his impossible son.

Creasy and Hicks were not only an old and reputable firm of lawyers, the senior partner, Hicks, was a parishioner of my father. Once the appropriate fee had been paid, I was taken into the firm as an articled clerk.

It was a return to cloud-cuckoo land. I did make a pretence of examining 'abstracts' and spilt ink over a number of valuable documents. I liked the other clerks. But legal conceptions turned remotely upon themselves beyond the reach of my intellect or imagination. They could never bring me back to reality and I continued to disintegrate.

After a week or two there was always a half bottle of gin in my desk drawer from which at frequent intervals I would take a good swig to the horror of Mr. Ridge, the old senior clerk, musty, rusty and with a high white collar. The younger articled clerks would join in at times and our room became quite lively. Hicks noticed.

'Do mark my words, Mr. Blackburn, the law is a serious calling. If you offer all you have to it, then the return will be infinitely rewarding. But it is a demanding profession. It has no time for malingerers.'

I agreed. But the spectator in the unconscious had planned to get me out of this and quite rightly decided my only exit was by disaster.

Normal young people went to parties and my parents were determined to believe I was normal. So parties! As I was rapidly tipping over into nightmare, the result was not happy.

'You are blonde and it is through a blonde mist that I see you. Goddess, together we will ascend, together, burning into the empyrean. We have, through innumerable lives, worked for this. Beatitude (yes, another glass, please), beyond argument or the fantasy of separate being, you and I, you and I . . .'

'You are a poet, Thomas.'

'You are the Word made flesh, and since I change flesh into words, we are made for each other.'

'Oh dear, I think he's going to be sick!'

'After such knowledge . . . what forgiveness?'

'He's passing out, do something, somebody!'

This is a strange bed, I do not recognize the wall paper or the pictures.

'Here's a cup of tea, it should make you feel better.'

'I'm so sorry!'

'No need, dear. You weren't sick on the carpet. No harm's done.'

That's a comfort. I am retching yellow bile into a flowered chamber pot.

'I am sorry for his sisters and parents.'

'Of course, he's not responsible.'

Do you not understand that I cannot rise till Easter?

'What must the Canon feel.'

'Weel may the keel row!'

I cannot rise till Easter.

On, on, on. Then the final party. Adelaide and Eliel have gone for a respite to Scarborough – they must have needed it – but my sisters and I have decided to 'entertain'. Half the county is coming but I am well away before the first guests arrive.

This is a form of death but is it necessary to go on pretending to be human? 'Sylvia, why do you look at the muck on the bed like that?'

'*Soyez sage.*'

'It is irrelevant, though I see you and your friend seeing. Whatever is covered by skin and a dinner jacket is stained with vomit.'

Next day my parents returned and learning of my performance
at this ultimate party decided that something must be done. Dr
Buchanan was called in. Some days later I was dispatched for
Brookfield Hall. This refuge for the alcoholic and narcotic-squad
and the moderately insane had some reputation. It had been
patronized by Royalty.

# Chapter Fourteen

We are closed in and the key is turned
On our uncertainty . . .

W. B. Yeats

The day before my departure at the age of twenty-three for Brook-field Hall, I bought all the writings of Freud and D. H. Lawrence I could get hold of in a Newcastle bookshop, and told Dr. Buchanan that my sole chance lay in a course of psychiatric treatment. He was reassuring.

'You'll get that, laddie,' he announced, 'and more besides. Brookfield is a fine place, you couldn't have a better.'

After a lugubrious train journey, Mother and I taxied to the Hall. A remarkable estate; the walls of old red brick were topped, appropriately enough, with broken bottles, and there were stone dragons on guard by the iron gates. We pulled an ancient bell reminiscent of Dracula's castle and a porter appeared. He touched his cap. 'Sir, Madam?'

'I am Mrs. Blackburn and this is my son. He has come for a short visit.'

'Quite so, Madam – we have been informed. I will open the gates and you may drive straight up to the Hall.' Charon brought out an enormous key and opened the portals. We drove up an admirable avenue of beech trees, past an ornamental lake tricked out with the wooden façade of a stone bridge, past a riding stables, a lawn on which some well-upholstered men and women were playing croquet and so to the front door. It was opened by a 'Kensitas' butler.

He bent forward from the hips and announced, 'You are expected, Madam. Be good enough to follow me and I will conduct you to the consulting room and inform the Medical Director of your arrival.'

Whatever hopes I had of treatment were dispelled when Dr. Mortimer came on the scene. The syndicate in charge of Brookfield had made the place extremely comfortable. No one could complain of the croquet lawn, the riding stables, the central heating, the billiard table, the hot and cold water in each bedroom – but effective medical treatment scarcely existed. Why should it? The rich families who sent their relatives to the place had paid a lot of money and had no desire for their speedy and disturbing return. The 'eccentrics' seemed to stay on indefinitely. The alcoholic and narcotic squad were kept out of circulation as long as possible. Not that Mortimer was a cut-price job; he had been to an excellent school, came of a good family and except when drunk, had very nice manners.

He was large, rotund, bibulous, hearty and wore a monocle. He had, I suspect, never read anything except the *Field*, *Sporting Life* and *Debrett* since his qualification as a doctor some thirty years previously. But although unfamiliar with anti-depressive drugs, any new methods of sedation or psychiatry, Mortimer did play a first-rate game of billiards. He was strong too, and could whisk on a very brisk strait-jacket when occasion demanded. His treatment of alcoholics and narcotics was identical. Shots of strychnine and hairs of the dog that bit you, controlled, but liberal and frequent. I do not believe he had ever effected a cure in his life or had any desire to do so. Why should he? Brookfield was a business concern and the point was to keep everyone on as long as possible. It is true that the alcoholics did go off at regular intervals, but they usually returned sodden and shaking for another 'dry out'.

'Well, young fellow,' Mortimer boomed, 'spot of trouble, eh? Never worry, we'll soon have you straightened out.' He didn't look really happy about me though. I was not the Brookfield type. But Mother was reassured, Mortimer had a somewhat Fenwicky look about him.

I had no confidence or hope at all until Nurse McCleod appeared. She was intelligent, resolute and Scottish. She looked at me in amazement.

'What in the name of Heaven are you doing here, young man?'
'Our doctor, Dr. Buchanan, recommended the place.'

'Dr. Buchanan, well, all I can say is that even if he's a Scotsman, he's a damned fool.'

'Why, nurse?'

'You're not an imbecile, that's obvious enough. You're not on "coke" or heroin. They tell me you drink, but you're not the kind of alcoholic we look after in this establishment, God help them.'

'*Lux perpetua luceat ei.*'

There had been Colonel Phillips, but Nurse McCleod was the first person who saw the way out of my confusion and set me on it.

'You should see Dr. Crichton-Miller. He's a friend of mine and I'll look after it. Oh, there's that damn' woman.'

Muffled by the thick Georgian ceiling but sharp enough for all that, a loud imperative scream came from the room above me. It was the Honourable Mrs. Payne, exceedingly rich, a relic of the 'gay' twenties, a heroin addict. With 'Dinner's at seven,' Nurse McCleod whisked upstairs. There was the sound of broken glass, two or three thuds, the voice of Dr. Mortimer, another short scream, a quieter one, then silence.

At six-forty-five the gong sounded and I trailed down a wide oak staircase to the dining-room. Halfway down, a small tea-rose of a man beautifully turned out and with whisky breath, poked his head out of a door.

'Psst, you're the new boy here, eh? Come in, we've just time for a "shorty".'

This scion of a well-known ship owning family had one of the finest suites. Innumerable silver and gold bottles of perfume decorated his dressing-table.

'Nice, eh, my little place? Had it done out myself – (it was covered with stripes of pink and mauve) – 'can't bear single colour walls – frowsty. Now I know what it's like to be a new boy here, was one myself, but that's many terms ago. Well, I'll tell you a secret – you're going to be my fag.'

He seemed quite safe. 'And very nice too,' I replied. The little man beamed with pleasure, 'Yes, isn't it, we must look after each other. Now what will it be, Scotch, Irish, gin, or will you have a very nice brandy?'

'Scotch, please.'

He took down a large bottle labelled 'Chanel Number 1', and murmuring, 'I think you'll find this the right stuff,' filled up two large tooth mugs.

'Well, chin chin and all that, and now we'd better skedaddle or Old Mortimer – he's Headmaster here, may give us a wigging!'

Mortimer was just embarking on grace and gave us a dirty look. He prided himself on his prayers and liked a full and attentive house.

'Your place is over there, Mr. Blackburn' – he pointed to a small flower-set table – 'and now let us stand for grace.

'Lord God, who has given to us thy children, wind and sky, health and hill' – (Mortimer was well-oiled that evening and in praying form) – 'hedgerow and ploughland, look down upon us.'

Twenty or so flushed faces looked up tolerantly at the doctor. They rather enjoyed his flights of fancy and it gave them a feeling of solidarity when he was 'sloshed'.

'Teach us thy children to enjoy thy simple gifts, the crystal water thou hast provided for our refreshment, the harmless fruits of the field, the company of bird and beast . . .'

'Bong, bong, bong,' the sporting reference had been too much for the sober but eccentric son of Lord Ulchester and he was firing left and right with both barrels of his fish-knife. The butler loomed forward and murmuring to Ulchester's delight that there was far better sport in another coppice led him from the dining-room.

Mortimer hardly noticed the interruption.

'O Thou who hast created the wind on the heath . . .'

'And my arse, Mortimer, and my bloody arse . . .'

It was Mrs. Payne – very high indeed, but to my surprise as she rambled through the room – boneless, apparently, transfigured by her penultimate injection, and nearing her table ground out her cigar in the eye of a cherubic caryatid of the mantelpiece, no one moved and the doctor continued. The guests of Brookfield did have a sense of decorum.

'The simple blessings of life, the water in which we swim, and bathe our bodies, which are the temples of thy Holy Spirit, the odour of new bread – friendship . . .'

'O belt up, you cunt, you've never had a friend in your life.' Mrs.

Payne spat reflectively into a tub of aspidistras and sat down at her table. As the grand-daughter of an earl who was kept from the bosom of her family by a very large sum indeed, she was not to be trifled with. However, Mortimer was almost finished.

'For these simple things, O Lord' – (with a salacious look at the jug of whitish liquid beside him; it was certainly not water) – 'make us truly thankful. Amen.'

We relaxed at our separate tables and I watched Mrs. Payne. Her 'shot' was wearing off, but she was worth looking at. A black dress, as negligible as it was expensive, sheathed her elegant, emaciated body. Her mouth was vermilion, her face chalk white, her red hair had long since died of heroin. I could see the syringe punctures on her thin bare arms. Early that morning I heard Dr. Mortimer scurrying along the corridor as she screamed in the room above me. He was paid tolerably well and at Brookfield there were . . . compensations, but Mrs. Payne made his life by no means easy. She was not reconciled to her addiction.

Next morning, the atmosphere was that of a well-run club and clinic for nursing mothers. At nine-forty-five the alcoholics and narcotics visited the consulting room of Dr. Mortimer in order of seniority. The former were given an injection of strychnine and a large medicine bottle of whisky or brandy; the latter strychnine and a shot of heroin, morphine or cocaine. The one rule was no convivial drinking. You took your bottle to the bedroom, knocked it back, then returned to circulation. I found the idea of enduring the tedium of Brookfield, and at ten a.m. with my senses exacerbated by alcohol, quite intolerable and refused my bottle, though I did let Mortimer squirt in the strychnine.

'If you've come here for a cure, then you must have treatment,' he announced, putting the yellow bottle labelled 'Guest 25, Room No. 17' back on the shelf.

After 'treatment' and breakfast, began a very serious business indeed – the motion.

Round the billiard table, or if the weather was clement, the croquet lawn, the gentlemen of Brookfield perambulated.

'How's it going this morning, Rawlings. Bad, eh? I'm stiff, very stiff indeed.'

'Bunged up to hell, old boy. It's those kidneys and beans they gave us last night, binding, very binding. Excuse me if I let off wind.'

He volleyed and thundered.

'Better now, Charles. Nothing like a good blow out. Remember Newsome – he was like a thirty-pounder.'

'You mean old Eddie Newsome, Mrs. Meyrick's pet. Excuse me, I think I'll have a go. That's better. Think I'm almost ready to pay a visit. Cheerybye. See you.'

I had no knowledge of Eddie Newsome but was terrified of these people who were identified with a motion of the bowels, the alcohol they absorbed, their shots in the arm. Still, watching them circulate the billiard table after a night made memorable by the screams of the Honourable Mrs. Payne, I think I became an addict at one remove and, knowing so much of it, incapable of real addiction.

The Hall catered for the rich passive addict who desired neither sex, conversation, violence, only a regulated supply of a drug in the context of a well-ordered womb. The formality of the place was remarkable, and perhaps of some therapeutic value. Whether one was mildly insane, an alcoholic or drug-addict, appearances were kept up. In the morning tweed suits or hacking jackets with cavalry twill trousers were worn by the men. The women, with the exception of Mrs. Payne who seldom appeared in the morning, but if she did, wore slacks or pyjamas, sported two-piece tweeds and sensible brogues. For tea, after the medicinal 'slug', or 'shot', it was lounge suits and tea-gowns. Even Mrs. Payne dressed for dinner. This concern reminded me of the cloacal obsession.

Although the 'guests' were puzzled that I had not been to a major public school, they found my youth, if not my company, reassuring. I was the youngest inhabitant ever and gave them the comfortable feeling that they were 'stayers' who had fought the good fight far more resolutely than myself. Unfortunately, though often buttonholed by some well-upholstered fellow addict, I could play neither bridge, pool nor snooker and found the unending accounts of binges at Mrs. Meyrick's 39 Club very boring, I was interested in their accounts of bowel motion, it had a certain psychological point. Offering nothing to society, like babies, the guests thought of their faeces as a valuable gift. But they did not enjoy my queries, and on other topics it was difficult to hide my boredom. I was soon ignored. Good. I read D. H. Lawrence and Freud as if my life depended on them. I walked for long hours, alone, through the grounds of Brookfield, my despair relieved once by a superb cock-pheasant shining in the November sun, an image perhaps of that unquenchable phoenix some element of myself still believed in. I also cocked an eye at various flaws in the Hall's defences and would from time to time loosen myself up with a medicinal whisky for a talk with La Payne.

She was no fool that one, and brightest at about five-thirty when she had received her major 'shot'. We met in a well-heated conservatory of tropical plants – an appropriate setting. As she lolled back in a wicker chaise-longue and chatted, I would listen, entranced not so much by her unending condemnation of the defects of her various husbands, as by the great drugged eyes of the woman and a mouth that seemed painted on an almost naked skull of extreme delicacy. Not that Payne's conversation was particularly enlightening. She described her first husband, Giles, as 'a very good rape' but did not enlighten me as to the defini-tion. Poor Giles had no concern for the imaginative delicacy of her sex. Her second, though extremely rich, was more devoted to his pack of fox-hounds and would from time to time spend a night in their company. Her third was a homosexual interior-decorator of some renown. He did understand 'what it is to be a woman' and although he was unable to consummate his marriage to Mrs. Payne, he did get her on to heroin. Imagination quickened. Surely I combined imaginative sensitivity and some sexual prowess. Our disparity of age was only twenty years or so. On me lay the duty of restoring her to a good, healthy life, and she would help me back into circulation. It was as simple as that. The capacity for fantasy is without limit.

To my surprise there was a stir of new life at Brookfield in the second week of December: Yule-tide was approaching and the girls and boys got busy with a Christmas tree and decorations. If you can't go forward, you must go back. The enthusiasm of my fellow guests for this Christmas festival was a return to their happier childhood before the bottle and the needle took them over. Dr. Mortimer, good soul, entered into the festive spirit and would often issue double rations. With a benevolent if nervous eye we watched Captain Forsythe balancing up one step ladder, John Ewebanke another, between them a cable of paper roses. When Montague Swithin, elevated by a double ration of Scotch, pitched from a chair on a table as he tried to fix silver stars to the candelabra and broke his arm, Mortimer celebrated the accident by a dinner-time speech not inappropriate to some war-time hero.

Because of her great wealth, and supreme connections, Mrs. Payne was in command of the Christmas tree. She supervised its decoration with regrettable levity.

'Now who shall we have at the top, an angel or baby Jesus?' She chose a remarkably naked and unpleasant celluloid doll and clipped it to the tree-top.

'There we are, meek and mild and without a stitch. What could be nicer?'

In those almost intolerable days I was delighted by Mrs. Payne's witticisms and, believing she was my soul mate, decided to press my suit on Christmas Eve. We were to have a real dinner party, all together round one table, with crackers and orangeade. Tension mounted. The day wore on. I decided that more Dutch courage was needed than could be supplied by a medicine bottle and after six almost teetotal weeks, climbed over the wall, darted to a nearby pub and, since as a guest of Brookfield I had no money, bartered my expensive teddy bear coat for a bottle of whisky. Half of the stuff was finished when I returned but I hid what remained in the conservatory and soldiered off to the dining-room. It was Mrs. Payne I was after.

Mortimer was well away that Yule-tide evening, soup was scarcely finished when, unable to contain his eloquence, he boomed, 'On this most happy occasion a few words are demanded of me.'

'They certainly are not,' said Payne. 'Sit down and don't make an ass of yourself. Mortimer, you're blotto!'

He was beyond such idle comment.

'This my friends, I must call you friends, my dear, dear friends, is the eve of Christmas. At Christmas we celebrate the birth of a child. Not just any child, no indeed, it is a very special baby we remember this very special evening. It is God's birthday. We celebrate the baby son of God.'

Mortimer bent down and took a good swig from the mug at his elbow. 'A little child, dear friends, but God for all that. God is beyond conceit, he is content to be born in the most lowly of all forms . . .'

'It's high time you were borne to bed,' said Payne, but was hushed by the guests. They were enjoying the oration.

'A king, the greatest of all kings, the son of the King of Heaven . . .'

'Wait for it, boys,' chirruped Payne.

'He is not born in a palace, He is not born in a mansion, He is not even born in a house. He is born in the humblest of all places, a manger. No bed but the respectable, I mean the receptacle, from which the cattle of the fields take their nourishment. There is a meaning for us all in this. It is not to the proud, the receptable . . . the respectable, that this child, this Christ child has come, but to the lost, the rejected, even to you, my dear friends, the riff-raff of this world!'

That wasn't a hit. Captain Forsythe went a very deep red and half rose from his seat. Cough, cough, cough, handkerchiefs! To be told, and after two weeks of hard decorating, that they were riff-raff, lost and rejected, did not appeal to Mortimer's guests. Despite certain lapses, they were eminently respectable. But they were tolerant of their own lapses. And it was by a lapse that the doctor redeemed himself.

'God bless you,' he announced, 'my dear friends. God bless you. Now I call upon you to rise for the loyal toast.'

The whole table rose to its feet chuckling. Mortimer was not only drunk, but had made a gaffe that would be remembered for a long time. He had proposed the loyal toast before the soup and it made our evening.

'One must give it to the old boy,' Forsythe remarked when we were reseated. 'He is one of us.'

It was Payne I was after. When dinner was over, I whisked off to the conservatory, took a good pull from my hidden bottle, and returned to the lounge. She was not there. My heart sank until I saw her lissom figure swaying towards me. She had been upstairs for a recharge and looked radiant.

'Shall we go into the conservatory?' I murmured with an expression and tone of voice intended to convey a passion which though sensual was deeply spiritual.

'All right . . . but how are you feeling?'

If every grain of insight I possessed had not been dissolved in alcohol, I would have seen she was not looking at me with rapture and delight, but a consternation which teetered on the edge of blind panic. Mrs. Payne had deep-seated and complex troubles which she tried to escape by heroin. I followed her into the conservatory and when she was settled in the chair of reminiscence, positioned myself on the carpet, my head close to one bony knee. She drew back with a shudder of repugnance which I took to be a sigh of passionate desire. I got on my knees and tried to kiss her. That did it. She screamed, ducked past me, raced through the lounge and drawing-room, still screeching, and was upstairs and battering on Mortimer's door. When he woke up and opened it, Payne flung herself into his arms sobbing, 'That brute, that filthy brute, he tried to rape me!'

The good doctor was deeply shocked. In his fifteen years at Brookfield nothing like this had ever happened. His guests did break out now and again; they shot off to London, or the nearby market town and after a few days or hours returned, in a taxi or ambulance maybe; but with dignity. They were ladies and gentlemen and did not make passes at each other.

I was 'out' myself by this time and only learnt of his wrath the morning after, from Nurse McCleod.

'After some searching of heart,' she beamed down at me, 'our good doctor has decided that you are to leave his little community. Young man, you should thank God to be out of it.'

# Chapter Fifteen

To Carthage then I came
Burning
O Lord thou pluckest me out
Burning.

T. S. Eliot

Nurse McCleod beamed at my hangover from behind the break-fast tray.

'Congratulations, Thomas, you proposed to me three times last night, and you got yourself expelled from this dump. It's never happened before.'

'I'm very sorry, Nurse McCleod.'

'About what?'

'The proposals.'

'Nonsense, I was flattered. Listen to this though. It's almost eleven o'clock, though you probably don't realize it, and I've been busy. I phoned the vicarage; luckily the Canon was out – a bit of a tartar I gathered from your rantings last night – but I did get hold of your mother. She'll be down on Tuesday and I've arranged an appointment for you with Dr. Crichton-Miller on Wednesday. You do have difficulties, that I'm well aware of, but if any man can help you he's the chap.'

Our Christmas Eve conversation is a blank and I doubt whether I talked with this Scotswoman for more than twenty sober minutes. But she helped me from death into life and in our short meeting we achieved the understanding of a lifetime.

The drawing-room of Oak Tree House, the consulting room of Brookfield, the room of Dr. Crichton-Miller in Wimpole Street; once again with her unfaltering if misguided devotion Adelaide is beside me. I suspect that Miller was in his own way a brilliant psychiatrist. I suspect formulae and believe that whether a follower of Freud or Jung a psychiatrist can only excel in his own way. Miller looked at and through me, swathed as I was in that horrible teddy bear coat which Mother had bought back from the publican and later adapted for her own uses. He looked at Mother, he looked back at me, he snorted then drawled:

'Well, young man, you have had every chance, you have good devout parents, and what a mess you have made of your life!'

It was a bold and intelligent approach. He wanted to find out, to see behind the mask. But at first I did not realize that his eyes, both friendly and acutely interested, bore no relationship to his hectoring question. I did feel a tingling in my hands and a tightening of the scrotum. Miller was summoning to his consulting room twenty-five years of pent-up fury against an attempt to nullify whatever is signified by 'life' and 'spirit'.

'You heard what I said, Blackburn; have you no sense of responsibility, no concern for others. What are you up to?'

The tingling and tightening increased.

'I want to get out of all this. I want to go to the colonies.'

'And what, pray, would you do in the colonies? Continue to sponge on your parents?'

I leapt for Miller's throat, roaring. Although about fifty-five, Miller, an agile rock-climber, slid past me and with a sweep of his arm knocked me, cursing, into a chair. The curses stopped when I looked at him and saw no condemnation, only compassionate interest. He had made his diagnosis and had another job now. It was to persuade Adelaide, in terms that would not disturb her, that her son needed treatment, and so preserve me from an asylum for the insane.

'Your son, Mrs. Blackburn, is over-sensitive, over-bred, a young man of great potentiality, but – pardon my asking this question – he was of course born during the war?'

This was right up Mother's street, she bridled with reassurance and pleasure.

'Not only that, doctor, three or four days before he was born, his birth place, Hensingham, was bombarded by the Germans from a submarine!'

Dr. Miller was delighted by this bit of nonsense. He could use it to get me treatment and bent forward in his chair.

'There we have it, Mrs. Blackburn, there we have it!'

'I always thought so, the boy was born under great stress.'

'Of course, he was. One can hardly think what the sensitive organism of a child has to suffer under the stress of war – and a bombardment just before his birth. This young man has got to be helped.'

He took out a pad, wrote down an address and handed it to Adelaide.

'I am going to ask you to send him to a colleague of mine, a really brilliant doctor. Dr. Hansom will be able to help your son more than myself. He is . . .'

With real understanding Dr. Crichton-Miller forestalled just those suspicions which Adelaide would have felt. Though a Rugby Blue and a D.S.O., Dr. Hansom was somewhat sallow and of Anglo-Prussian extraction. He was devoted to poetry, had no small talk but a remarkable capacity for silence.

'Dr. Hansom will not say much but believe me he will be better able to help your son than I can.'

That was true. Though Crichton-Miller's diagnosis of myself and handling of Mother were admirable, he was of an extrovert turn of mind and I doubt whether we would have shared that intuitive understanding necessary for a satisfactory analysis. I admire his impersonal care. I also admire Dr. Hansom's insistence that Mother should not stay with me in London.

'No, Mrs. Blackburn,' he repeated with determination, 'if you wish me to treat your son then you must leave him in London on his own. Yes, I do realize he may get into trouble. That is a risk we must take; but his being alone here is a condition of treatment.'

That Adelaide did agree to the terms of this skilled psychiatrist is to her credit. I was left to myself, in an extremely expensive hotel too. Though Mother had no lack of cash she was a trifle deficient in worldly wisdom and had no idea that boarding houses or furnished rooms existed.

Now the other journey began. After many years of blind and compulsive action I turned inwards to discover myself. It was not easy. When dissociated, death-wishing energies dominate the conscious mind, what occurs could well be explained by the diabolic possession of the New Testament. We know very little. I think that the Christ of the Gospels was often unconditioned by the climate of his particular time and place. When he talks of devils – they have no horns and tail, that is a later addition – He may well have used the most valid image for those death-wishing powers which can dominate us.

Dr. Hansom was the exorcist who summoned my 'demons' into a daylight of understanding where they could not, as themselves, continue to exist. Even Count Dracula must disintegrate if surprised by dawn. Incidentally it is significant that the Transylvanian gentleman had to bed down upon the coffined soil of his own country after each nocturnal expedition. Our present torments depend upon a fixation to the past.

Once Hansom had disturbed my 'demons', they fought desperately and with their own strong energy against the light in which they must suffer not death but transformation. There were alcoholic blackouts. I would walk from the couch in Harley Street dazed with revelation; with dissolution also since I was between two worlds, 'One dead, the other powerless to be born'. I knew; but I saw no way out of the confusion into which I had gained some insight. A false exit was the nearest bar or nightclub. Since the 'demons' also found the insight I had gained in Harley Street intolerable, after a few whiskies and a brisk skirmish between the backward intention and my new understanding, I would pass out.

The demons remain; but they are taken up and changed by some unguessed-of, life-serving intention. After a few weeks I realized that I must know, realized with the certainty of conversion. For weeks on end I would sit in my room and read Schopenhauer, Bergson, Blake, Plato, Nietzsche as if my life depended on gaining knowledge – which it probably did. There were occasional bouts of chaos from which I gained only oblivion and a hangover – but the reading – reading and analysis continued.

After about six months my parents were disturbed by my long stay in London and I went North to ask for further time.

'But you can't go on like this for ever, dear.'

'I do need more time with Dr. Hansom, Mother. I don't want to slip back again, I must go on.'

'You should want to do something though, get a foothold on real life, start work again.'

Begging the question of the value of any work I had done, at least in the legal sphere, I used cunning. When the pressure to stop my analysis by withholding cash reached 'flash point', I would close my eyes and start to tremble; the trembling increased in violence until Mother softened up.

'It's all right, dear, it's all right, you shall go back to London and continue your . . . treatment.'

The strategy was effective and after some years I reached the state of moderate lucidity and direction which ends this story.

I have tried to explore, through my parents, myself and others, the pattern made by certain benighted energies of thought and feeling as they work themselves out in a family. Generation after generation the lives of a family can be determined by what we call neurosis and the Greeks called a curse. When inhabited by this curse, men and women inflict great suffering upon themselves and other people. But since they are the creatures of the curse and unaware of its real nature, they may act out its destructive intentions with a sense of impeccable rectitude. One can note the patterns of behaviour, bizarre, and at times of extreme cruelty, but blame is irrelevant since the creatures of these patterns are unaware of the compulsion which determines their lives.

The curse on the House of Atreus ended when Orestes, under the protection of Apollo, that supreme exorcist, turned and confronted the Furies in open court. The Furies are always with us and, if we can confront them, serve the fulfilment of life. Since its purpose has been to show a life in flight from the Furies and in consequence dominated by them, this book is now finished. After about three years of analysis, I did come to some terms with my destiny and learn to use it. From that time on is another story.

# ALSO AVAILABLE FROM VALANCOURT BOOKS

MICHAEL ARLEN — Hell! said the Duchess
R. C. ASHBY (RUBY FERGUSON) — He Arrived at Dusk
FRANK BAKER — The Birds
WALTER BAXTER — Look Down in Mercy
CHARLES BEAUMONT — The Hunger and Other Stories
DAVID BENEDICTUS — The Fourth of June
PAUL BINDING — Harmonica's Bridegroom
CHARLES BIRKIN — The Smell of Evil
JOHN BLACKBURN — A Scent of New-Mown Hay
Broken Boy
Blue Octavo
The Flame and the Wind
Nothing but the Night
Bury Him Darkly
THOMAS BLACKBURN — The Feast of the Wolf
JOHN BRAINE — Room at the Top
The Vodi
MICHAEL CAMPBELL — Lord Dismiss Us
R. CHETWYND-HAYES — The Monster Club
ISABEL COLEGATE — The Blackmailer
BASIL COPPER — The Great White Space
Necropolis
HUNTER DAVIES — Body Charge
JENNIFER DAWSON — The Ha-Ha
BARRY ENGLAND — Figures in a Landscape
RONALD FRASER — Flower Phantoms
GILLIAN FREEMAN — The Liberty Man
The Leather Boys
The Leader
STEPHEN GILBERT — The Landslide
The Burnaby Experiments
Ratman's Notebooks
MARTYN GOFF — The Youngest Director
Indecent Assault
STEPHEN GREGORY — The Cormorant
JOHN HAMPSON — Saturday Night at the Greyhound
THOMAS HINDE — Mr. Nicholas
The Day the Call Came
CLAUDE HOUGHTON — I Am Jonathan Scrivener
This Was Ivor Trent
JAMES KENNAWAY — The Mind Benders
CYRIL KERSH — The Aggravations of Minnie Ashe

Lightning Source UK Ltd.
Milton Keynes UK
UKOW03f2126250314

228824UK00004B/215/P